DOs & DON'Ts

Also by
Suroosh Alvi, Gavin McInnes, and Shane Smith

The Vice Guide to Sex and Drugs and Rock and Roll

DOs & DON'Ts

10 YEARS OF *VICE* MAGAZINE'S STREET FASHION CRITIQUES

WARNER BOOKS

NEW YORK   BOSTON

Warner Books

Time Warner Book Group
1271 Avenue of the Americas, New York, NY 10020
Visit our Web site at www.twbookmark.com.

Printed in the United States of America

First Edition : September 2004
10 9 8 7 6 5 4

Library of Congress Cataloging-in-Publication Data

ISBN: 0-446-69282-4
LCCN: 2004108724

For Emily

10 YEARS OF BEING MEAN

An interview with the author of *VICE*'s DOs & DON'Ts.

Vice: Who writes the DOs & DON'Ts?
Gavin McInnes: I've always written them but the reason this book has three names on the byline is DOs & DON'Ts wouldn't exist without the three of us. Suroosh founded the company and is the one that got us this book deal and Shane's been handling the business side of VICE Magazine and everything else since day one. This book isn't like Judy Blume sitting down by herself to write a book and having her editor give comments along the way. The writing is only a small part of it. DOs & DON'Ts is the result of a lot of people's hard work. Our photographers, for example, come from all over the world. The final result is really a group effort. It's like a gang bang where I'm the one getting fucked.

What?
I don't know.

How would you define a DON'T?
I don't know. I guess it's someone that is trying really hard and not pulling it off, someone that has no sense of humor about it. And then a DO would be someone with an innate sense of style that doesn't even have to try. But then there's times when I'll just stick a DO in the DON'Ts because we have too many DOs that month. Like I put this Lizard Man in the DON'Ts even though I think it's pretty ballsy to become a freak for life like that. He covered his whole body in green scale tattoos and split his tongue down the center and I'm calling that a fashion faux pas? Often there's no difference between DOs and DON'Ts. It's just whatever works better.

How do you come up with the comments?
What kind of question is that? I lay out the best pictures and think of funny things and then write them down. How do you come up with the questions?

One thing I can't help but notice is you're not that great of a dresser yourself. Aren't you from Canada?
Yeah, those are both true. I dress like a homeless mod from the 70s and, in Montreal, that's considered incredibly stylish. I guess the point of a lot of these commentaries is fashion doesn't matter. I mean, I hate looking at metrosexuals wearing flip flops with a suit but I usually get over it when they walk out of view. It's only annoying for a very short time. The truth is fashion is boring and only really stupid people genuinely care about it.

I'm always surprised how many girls like the DOs & DON'Ts. It's done from such a male perspective.

Yeah, but that's not ideal. I want it to be as genderless as possible. I get around it with things like, "I'm no fag but I'd let this guy lick my balls while I jerk off" or even, "I'm going to take a pill to become gay so I can marry this guy." I think that helps dull down the male perspective but one of the reasons I think women enjoy reading the DOs & DON'Ts is actually because it's from a male perspective. Not a gay male perspective or a women's perspective like most fashion critiques. I remember one of the editors at Bust telling me her and her friends really appreciated the DO where I talked about how hot it is when girls wear black socks with sneakers. I think she said something like, "We had no idea you guys liked that." Most women have no idea how weird most guys' tastes are and I think the DOs & DON'Ts sheds some light on that.

Have you ever gotten sued or beaten up?

No, just hassled. One time we had this douchebag in a Montreal café working on his computer in the DON'Ts. I said something about how "gay" that is and a group called the Quebec Association of Gay Journalists (or something) told us we were being investigated. I tried to explain it was the fourth-grade "gay" meaning "lame" but that made them even more mad. They said, "Once again de Henglish are trying to dismiss hate speech towards de French by saying we don't understan deir language." There was no arguing with them, though I tried for a long time. I even pretended I was gay and I think there was some flirting going on. Anyway, a few weeks later we received a notice that we had been deemed homophobic but I still don't know what this decision means. I think it was just one guy posing as an organization and smashing a gavel down in his bedroom to feel important.

Another time we had this Jamaican guy in the DOs and he was furious. I had to talk to that guy for hours and hours. He didn't care about the comment (it was some joke about Quebeccers and it was in French so he couldn't understand it). His problem was simply being photographed. I tried to tell him the whole, "When you are in a public place there is a reasonable expectation you will be photographed" thing but he wasn't having it. "What if I was commitin' a crime Kebin?" he kept saying (he called me Kebin). I couldn't understand what point he was trying to make. Criminal privacy rights? I told him I'd buy him lunch and he could have some CDs and a T-shirt or something and he was like, "Oh no Kebin, it's going to be a lot more than a T-shirt. I got Babylon closin' in on me and I am going to get some com-pohn-saye-tion!" He even got a fucking lawyer. When the lawyer called me I had to explain that the dude was in the DOs and the charge was basically "public flattery" and I could tell that threw him off a bit but he still tried to get some cash. Lawyers are cocksuckers.

Besides that it's all been pretty mild. They're always ridiculous complaints. People take themselves way too seriously. One guy was angry about being in the DOs because, as he put it, "I like to be in control of my image." What?

Are you at least sympathetic to some of these people?

Are you? How can they be serious? We had this Buddhist swastika in the DON'Ts that I photographed in Taiwan and I pretended I was outraged at the Chinese for making a mockery of the victims of WWII and we had hundreds of people telling us to "do our research" because it wasn't a nazi restaurant—it was a Buddhist restaurant. Um, doye, you think we thought it was a fucking nazi restaurant? What do they serve there SS burgers and "Orange Jews"?

I also don't have any sympathy for people that complain about "hate speech" and words like "cunt" or "nigger." Those are swear words. You swear when you're making jokes. It's funnier that way. If you're so concerned about politics then why the fuck are you taking up arms to fight a comment about someone's pants? There's better forums for political battles than your pants.

I think the people that get angry about this stuff fall into two groups. The first are puritans. They get shocked by some sexual reference and pretend it's because the reference was sexist but what they really mean is, "You shocked me." The other group are academics and rich kids that like to patronize people. They pretend they're offended by your misunderstanding of a swastika but what they really mean is, "I'm sophisticated and you're not."

Boring. How come you never name the celebrities you put in there?
Because that is so fucking lame. Those party pictures at the back of magazines where you have Moby hanging out with Adrian Brody at some terrible promo party with plastic cups of shitty champagne are the worst things on earth. It's way more fun to ignore celebrities. Besides, I think people enjoy guessing who they are.

What are your favorite DOs & DON'Ts?
I never really know which one is a hit until people say it is. The baby with the purple track pants that I called a fat bitch was probably the most popular one. And the guy who masturbates listening to Massive Attack. That one did well. I think my favorites were the ones we did with Joe Strummer. He really got it. It's all about pretending to give a shit what people wear and he managed to do that perfectly. I never found out what he thought about the first book. Too bad he died.

What do you hope to achieve with the DOs & DON'Ts?
A lot of shit. A lot. First I'd like to be responsible for the end of sandals. Especially on men. I'd also like it if I contributed to a ban on men's toes in general. I am fucking sick to death of looking at men's toes. I'd also like to see them stop waxing their chests and getting pedicures. Men aren't supposed to look pretty. Have you ever seen a bag? That's proof. As far as women go I'd like them to learn that we don't really give a shit if they're fat and have droopers. We don't like make-up or perfume so stop wasting all your money on it. If a woman wears high heel shoes and dresses even a little slutty, we're in. Also, I want all those purple loving people to know that purple is the color of sexual frustration and we are laughing at how horny they are. Then I'd like to get some people with babies out of my face. That's about it.

Do you use the DOs & DON'Ts to get laid?
I remember asking a famous guy if he uses his job to get laid and he looked at me incredulously, pointed to his face and said, "Well, this ain't cutting it!" I use whatever I can to get laid. That's the thing about having full blown AIDS with severe genital warts covered in herpes. You need an angle.

Um, what's with the cartoon underwear?
Originally I was nude in this photograph but the people at Warner Books said it would kill sales. They said guys wouldn't buy the book. After talking about it with them for awhile I kind of agreed so we cut it out.

Any last words?
I'd like to thank some of the more regular photographers. Alain Levitt did a lot of the really posed DOs you see here. Tim Barber did a lot too. So did Jodie Abrams and Vito Fun. Alex Cooley helped with the layout a lot. Colin Fox at Warner Books was a big part of this. Mostly, however, I'd like to really thank me for being there whenever I needed me.

Dude is just chilling. He's unflappable. You could be like, "Humpty, what if nobody shows up to our party?" and he'd be all, "Don't worry about it doood."

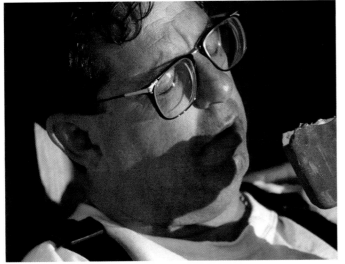

"Holy fuck, this ice cream is good. I have been jonesing for chocolate and vanilla since yesterday and now this bitch is in my mouth, melting between my teeth like a naked little whore. Jesus, God, it's better than taking a shit on heroin. I wish I could take my pants off right now I feel so fucking good. Uuuh."

One of the best places to dance like no one is watching AND meet hot women is the Royal Victorian Institute for the Blind's annual mixer. Right now he's a good-looking black man with a tasteful suit on.

What are you doing, you stupid, stupid bitch? Your long hair is gone. Let it go. Jesus. You think that irritating rat tail is some kind of memorial to all your hard hair work? I want to cut it off so bad it feels like I have to go pee.

Who's laughin' now, Bin Laden? You thought you could blow everyone up and then devastate the American economy and polarize the world and then escape, but we caught you. And we did it for no money with zero casualties. Now you're on death row in, um, Texas.

Hey, baby man. You don't need to put four things on your head (including two hats?), but if you do, you might not want to draw attention to yourself by picking the living shit out of your nose. We are all looking at you and thinking about your dad and condoms.

Dear fags,
If heteros get on your nerves so much, why don't you do something about it? Don't just sit there with a bottle of red wine bitching about how gross vaginas are and how breeders make you sick. Get out there! Find out where they do it! And go fucking fart on them!

Ki hal chelay, pyari lerki? They're kind of hard to handle during a heat wave but when it's really cold and rainy out, there's nothing like a big-titted fatso to get under the covers with. It's like eating a big meal after you've been chopping wood all day.

Besides the gay farter, every picture on this page was taken in a crowded bar. What is going on over here? Everyone is just fucking and sucking and pulling their tits out and people are slipping on the dancefloor because it's covered in jizz.

It's rad when you don't have to sit there guessing what her tits are going to be like. It's like, "These are my tits. Take 'em or leave 'em." The gays have been doing shit like that with weird codes (like which bandana is in which pocket) for years. We're finally up to the "no bullshit" stage.

Flat stomachs are an urban myth. Guys like a bit of a cunt gut because it's like a third tit and girls like a guy with a beer belly because it shows he cares about important stuff and doesn't spend all his time staring at the mirror, worrying about his figure. Fuck you, metrosexuals!

"Let me see here. What am I going to put on my dangling ball? Some kind of wee hat ... a paper cup? Ooooh, a golf-club cozy! Perfect."

If you want to get your tag out there you have to put it where people are going to see it, like on a big billboard near the highway or on a naked drunk girl at a party.

Dude, keep holding on to her and don't let go for the rest of your life. She is about seven miles out of your league and you are never going to have tits like that in your mouth ever again (ever).

"Don't no motherfuckers do anything in this town without talking to Captain Garbage first. I run the garbage in this town. If you got a problem with your garbage—somethin' you can't fix, well, you come have a sit down here with me in this garbage and I'm-a handle it. Simple as that."

This guy just looks like a good jam. I don't know what he's playing, if it's a Kurtis Mantronik remix of EPMD or something, but when you look at him you can almost hear the best song you've ever heard in your life.

This woman looks so much like a gerbil I really want to stuff her up my ass.

Dear Diary, I am so fucking bald right now I feel like I'm going to explode. I feel like the sun is looking down at me and thinking, "Holy shit, is that guy ever bald."

All your bad secrets. Everything you've ever done that you want to forget. Every silent fart you ever had. It's all in his hair. It's all in his bread dread portable bed that he carries everywhere he goes. That and billions and billions of tiny bugs.

You may have heard about how we're on this pro-puke tip these days but we mean it in a Roman way: to prevent you from getting too wasted. Not in a puke-on-the-bench-I'm-sitting-on-then-roll-in-it-then-try-to-get-up-but-fall-asleep kind of way.

Geez, why don't you just get a dead guy to stand outside holding a sign advertising cigarettes, or maybe a crack whore dying of AIDS can try to sell you a blow job. Oh wait, crack whores dying of AIDS *do* try to sell you a blow job.

"I can't believe this invisible spray actually works, honey! We can do whatever we want wherever we want without anyone seeing us. It's like the world is our living room."
Shut up and piss on me, Meghan.

"You know the fascinating thing is that magic was considered 'the work of sorcerers' a hundred years ago. If you were caught even making an egg disappear (which I just did) you would have your hair burnt off and your hands blackened. Now people would kill to see a good musician, I mean, magician but they can't...
Hello!? Are you even fucking listening to me?"

We are passionately against men wearing any toe-baring shoes, but this is an exception. This dude is so "going to the beach" it hurts the city's feelings.

OK here's another exception. You can get away with flip flops in the winter when you go and get ninja socks from Japan and rock them all "Fuck you" style.

Not since Mussolini has a straight male been able to pull off tidy and spotless without looking like a raging homo. The guy has a scarf and a fedora and he's still scary. Fuck.

When the balding Chinese lady in the sweatshop in Wisconsin was making this shirt she quietly thought to herself, "I have a feeling this shirt is going to go over the heads of our usual clientele and do really well in the Lower East Side." And the bitch was right!

GET HIM! Get him! Dude, he doesn't even really have you in a headlock. It's more of a head *squeeze*. Just keep doing that throat thing to his Adam's apple because it's fucking killing him (the little fag).

Good luck pulling off pig tails and hippie shirts when you're 35. But right now? Holy fucking mother of God. No wonder her boyfriend chugs whiskey. I'd be bawling my eyes out.

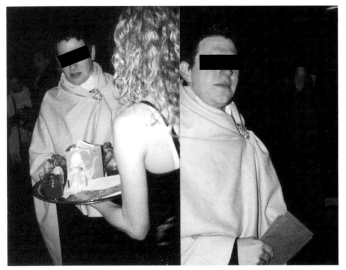

Look, I'm not saying we all have to dress like Lemmy, but a pink shawl with a yellow ascot and a hot-pink purse? His big brother must be looking back at all the wedgies he never gave and thinking to himself, "How did I let this happen?"

Having sleepovers at Rob Zombie's is the best because you get to hang out in his bar with your socks on and have pillow fights in the band room.

We're a very pro-barf publication. There's no sense in letting shots sit in your belly, getting you more drunk when you're already in bed. So, if your friend is too high just fucking grab her by the waist and SNAP her forward as hard as you possibly can. The centrifugal force is intense but she'll thank you for it tomorrow.

It can be a bit tricky coming back into the singles scene after 25 years of marriage. You can either buy *Cosmo* and try to figure out what the latest trends are or you can get your own shit goin' on! Your own "geriatric playboy drag king music teacher winter Robin Hood" shit goin' on!

He had car pajamas when he was ten. Then, because he went straight from his Mommy's bosom to his wife's, he got himself a Ferrari windbreaker suit. Grown up children need to be told to fuck off.

Now that goth is back, you're going to be seeing a lot more black and lace and... fuck I'm horny.

When people dress the same they send out a message to everyone around them and that message is, "We are in our own little world here, so fuck you." I got a better idea. How about fuck YOU. You are in your own little world because we banished you there. Don't pretend it was your idea.

"I am a butterfly. I am a black crow. I am a butterfly too. I am an asshole. [chorus] I'm that star up in the sky. I'm that mountain peak up high. I made it. I'm the world's greatest. And I'm that little bit of hope. When my back's against the ropes. I can feel it mmm. I'm the world's greatest."
-R. Kelly

The problem with anything ethnic or African is it can look totally contrived and insincere, like someone hiding the fact that they come from Akron. When someone pulls it off with this level of aplomb, however, they make all those fucking idiots in the "Status Headdress of Dagomba" look like naked Danny DeVitos dancing on the bar of a Harlem jazz club.

Punk wasn't actually like this back in the 70s and 80s. It was pajamas and beards and rubber boots but this is better. 2004 retro punk is better than the original. It's even better than 90s retro punk.

Did she just put out an album called *God Hates Us All*?! - because that outfit is Slaying me. The cleavage – no cleavage/ 80s shit is one thing but the matching boots and belt just put it into overdrive - shit.

This is sort of what the Prima Donnas sound like. It's that kind of big sister, French new-waver vibe.

If Anti-Pop Consortium and Outkast had a baby it would look like this. One of those outfits that, with the right amount of balls, can turn everyone else in the room into a pile of soft sand.

Nice fucking purple track pants, you fat bitch. What are you, the fucking Michelin Man? Nice gay hat, too, you fucking little loser bitch.

BERLIN: I don't know if you've ever been to a Nazi rally but there is inevitably one giant question that keeps poking and poking at your brain like an incessant thing: Who has better outfits, the Nazis or the people that are here to stop them? The Nazis have amazing graphic design skills and their outfits are neat as a pin. They've got the well polished boots with the perfectly tailored pants and puffy jackets and the vintage sunglasses…

BERLIN: The protestors, on the other hand, tend to rock more of a "grimy bandito" look that features a lot more colorful accessories and pins and fingerless gloves and all that with the kick ass "don't film me" anarchist face masks. You should have seen the riot that broke out after this. It was to die for.

  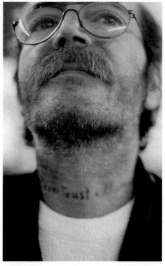

DUBAI: The thing about hot Arab bitches is, you know that underneath those black, polyester dresses they are wearing the Yves Saint Laurent classic heel with the ankle strap and a tiny Vivienne Westwood skirt that only her husband and his servants will ever get to see. Fuck, they're like walking Christmas presents.

LONDON: Finally, the drag queen ARE Weapons geriatric rabbit diva thing is back. What took you so long dude? I've felt like an idiot standing here trying to explain us to people.

MUNICH: Fucking right. You should "never trust a woman." Their pants are so on fire it's insane. Kudos to this German alcoholic for having the balls to get a gigantic neck tattoo that tells bitches exactly what the rest of us were too scared to say.

BEIJING: There is no excuse for a Chinese bum. Asians are supposed to be better than us (they don't even need chairs) and now you've got some guy lying on the ground with a hat that says, "spare change?" You can't even play some weird instrument? Fuck you and your waste of a superior brain.

OAKLAND: Hey, it's the guy from Snap! ("I've got the power!") but with a little more Dungeons and Dragons in him. He sees himself as an intense comic book version of *Friday Night Videos* but can you imagine what he'd do if he saw himself through our eyes? He'd puke from laughing.

ST JOVITE: Is Quebec run by babies? They deface stop signs because "stop" is an English word then, instead of going with the standard speed limit warnings, they make their own "our children could be yours" sign and draw a dead kid on the bottom with his fucking shoe blown off.

BRISTOL: Most of the hash in Britain has been smuggled from Amsterdam via Arabic men's asses. However, judging by the quality of the hash there these days it seems they stopped putting actual hash up there and now just come back from the airport, shit into a bag and say, "here."

DATONG: Hey red eyes, I know the people in this building are raising you for food and you're covered in blood from the other dogs because you went nuts all caged up in the sweltering heat but still, could you be more grossitating please? It's like, "Ew."

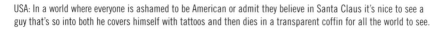

USA: In a world where everyone is ashamed to be American or admit they believe in Santa Claus it's nice to see a guy that's so into both he covers himself with tattoos and then dies in a transparent coffin for all the world to see.

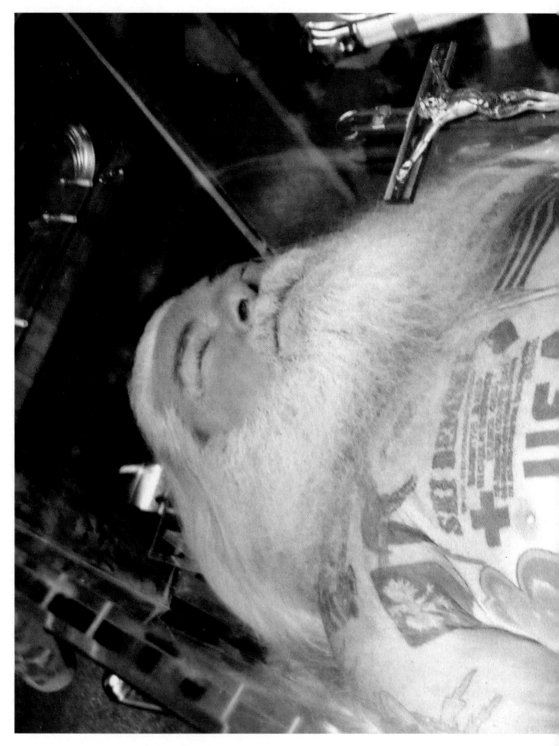

VANCOUVER: One great thing about the West Coast is the sheer hangoutability of the place. Taking a picture of your buddy wearing a huge pair of pants is considered having done something that day and it means you can go back inside and drink another six pack in front of the TV totally guilt free.

OAKLAND: We tend to shit on "Timmies" for using umbrellas on their bikes or selling wind chimes or having highlights in their hair but when dudes show some serious Timmy pride and make a whole lifestyle out of it—well—you can't really fuck with that.

GENOA: You know a city is paradise when you don't notice that the ground is covered in syringes, dudes are still heavily into grunge and every woman that you meet is totally fucking nuts.

SINGAPORE: The best thing about places with no crime is you just pick up a bike, hop on it and away you go. You can go see all the sites zipping through traffic like a little dude and then you get to your place and throw it down on the road like it ain't no thang. Next!

GLASGOW: Seeing a hot girl in Scotland is incredibly fucking rare. It simply doesn't happen. So when it does, and she's crass, and horny, and dresses well, it's kind of a catch 22 because you got so horny you shit your pants.

LAHORE: While all you Western moms are sitting around in Daniel Hector sweatshirts talking about taxes and then microwaving lasagne, Paki moms are in the mountains blowing people's heads clean off their shoulders. What's up now, bitch?

AMSTERDAM: I know you think this is a Chinese postcard or a still from a Karaoke video but we swear to god this male-model-for-virgins was actually sitting there being this guy. He's hot, but only to 4 year-old Asian girls or gay guys that have vaginas.

PARIS: France has breakfast and desert locked down but the part we hate is when you go to someone's house and everything is painted purple and orange and her fucking brother is listening to records with no fucking pants on. That part has got to go.

TAIPEI: Hey Taiwan, fifty million fucking people died in that war you assholes! You think that's a nice logo for a restaurant? What do you serve there, the dog from a few pages back? You are a bunch of gay fucking jerks and I hate your stupid guts.

STUTTGART: Having your children tortured to death by Israeli secret police sucks balls. Watching your Mother bleed to death on the street after a suicide bomber blew her leg off is also gay. But what about what I go through? I had to listen to this smug college boy piece of turd tell me how simple it all is to solve as he made German spaghetti.

LOS ANGELES: A lot of chiefs get into Krishna, not for the submissive women and the ethical food and all that, but for the chance to wear soft pajamas and totally fag out. Dude, you can make it as spiritual as you want. You still have a fucking kitten in your purse.

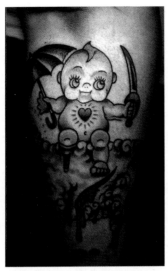

One time God appeared to me as a human and said, "If you look at the beach of life you will see two sets of footprints. You will also notice there is only one set when you were going through hard times. Those are mine. I was carrying you...er, hello?" And I was like, "I'm sorry, I'm sorry, I'm just having trouble paying attention because I can't stop staring at your tits."

And the winner of The Greatest Tattoo of All Time goes to... a heartwarming pirate baby, sitting on the three-eyed sheep he just stabbed, in the rain. Apparently the mayor of WTF!? was visiting the shop that day.

When you're having trouble getting laid and you want your friends to know it's getting on your nerves but you don't want her to know, invent some kind of way that your friends can see what's going on without her noticing. Then everybody wins.

Teenagers in Tokyo dress so good it's like they're magic babe fairies that come out of red bits of fudge and dance around you like a box of shimmer biscuits. It's not even a sex thing. Fucking them would be like raping Tinkerbell.

Ever have a blue flame where you're like, "This is going to be huge" and you get all your buddies together and you push like hell and you light it perfectly and it's like, "PRAAAAPPPFFF" and the flame is about 30,000 times better than you thought it was going to be? You're like, "I could die happy right now."

Sure my man Jay-Z got Beyoncé, but don't hate. That's just how my motherfucking niggas roll, dawg! Rocafella is all about the finest bitches and if a motherfucking bitch gets this shit you know the ho is down with The Roc. True dat!

Have you ever seen a fatter piece of shit in your life? Hey lardass, take it easy on the Mars Bars. You are basically a red-and-black sphere with brown hair on the top and silly shoes on the bottom.

Did you ever wonder where fashion trends come from? Did you think a computer spat them into a gay man's hands and he then turned them into pants and put them on a skinny girl who talks funny? No!
Fashion is invented by a really smart guy with a fanny pack named Scary Perry (left), who explains his ideas to a magic fairy (right) who puts the ideas in a huge red bag and drops them down the chimneys of expensive department stores. That is why this picture is worth two hundred million dollars. It's like a picture of the Wizard of Oz.

You know when you're really fucked up on acid and you end up carrying a thing around all night? Well, sometimes a guy will latch on to an item (like an owl) that ends up being so perfect, everyone else ends up looking at their thing (a deflated basketball, a brown hat, a kid's shoe) and going, "fraig" like a guy that married the wrong person.

Aw fuck. I showed up with my really old black friend thinking I was going to outdo everyone and then these girls show up with a cool abbo. Now I have to leave the party and try to find, like, an intellectual, black, German leprechaun dandy or something...

"Sorry, Mr. Pimples, though I understand your need to have unconventional friends as a fashion accessory, I am on a specific training regime. After several jaunts up and down Broadway I shall be spending the rest of the day ensconced in an armchair, reading *The Stuttgart Review*...alone! Good day and good luck."

With all due respect to the victims of the bombers in Falluja, this ass and the way it has been presented to the viewer (the boots and then—POW—the socks, and then—WHAM—the tights and then the shorts—BOOM!) is just as powerful as any loss any family has ever had in any act of war, ever—even Dresden.

Right on! You know what my passion is? Being forced to picture a gigantic, sweaty Greek man in black socks bouncing his hairy brown balls against this poor woman's ass for hours and hours and hours. On behalf of everyone fortunate enough to walk behind you, thanks!

What the fuck? Is this guy on a dare? He's got Jamaica-colored accessories and a shirt that essentially says, "Niggers can't fight," like he's in *Die Hard 3*.

He's like one of those drawings you pass around the table where one guy draws a fat Mexican head, the other guy draws a goth metal body, the next guy draws a racist drag-queen bottom, and the last guy just draws some funny boots because he can't really draw.

Hey, why don't you do the one about the junkie dad who's so desperate for smack he holds sock-footed concerts at his apartment where idiots pay £10 to hear him play songs from the band he just got kicked out of.

Of course, some dads don't even play guitar and have decided to raise money for drugs simply by not paying the rent. Sure your daughter's legs are in bird shit and there's spiders in her diapers, but you just saved six hundred bucks!

Thanks to Ashanti going all *Grease* on us in that Ja Rule video, there are now hundreds of black hip-hop chicks dressing like Sandy. They combine the Goody Two-shoes part with the slut-at-the-end part and the result is the whole reason God invented boners.

When my sister dropped out of school we talked about her becoming many things. She could have started her own clothing line or opened a record store or even learned to play bass and start a band. She could have done a lot of stuff, but in the end, she decided to focus on heroin and being a colostomy bag for some drunk guy's cum.

While the majority of us are speedily busting our nuts into gym socks, there are dudes who do it in the bath, toes pointed, legs in the air, Massive Attack blaring, ice cube in mouth, candles everywhere, and tons of scented oil on their balls. Eeeeeeeeeew.

Being the only black kid in Canadian kindergarten can be pretty harsh. When your dad comes from Papua New Guinea, and doesn't understand the implications of dressing you in a tiny monkey suit with a felt banana in the pocket, you're basically fucked for life.

What's better: fighting to the death for the land God gave you thousands of years ago OR that part of the night where the MDMA is just kicking in and the beat keeps building and building until it breaks into a "bkkkkkkkkkkkkkkkksheeaw" and everyone's cheering?

This is yet another one of those really old European guys who thinks simply moving to the artsy neighborhood and pretending to be eccentric is going to allow some 21-year-old virgin to accept his withered gray penis into her soft pink mouth.

OK, we're kind of hard on our hometown in the DON'Ts, but "Les Tam Tams" is just one tiny part of it—the shitbag hippie part. There are some great things about Montreal. Like just below St. Catherine's, where all the blind retards, 70-year-old Fonzarellis, shitfaced squaws, and geriatric lesbians spend their welfare checks on three-dollar pitchers.

It's stupid to go see the Sex Pistols now, because it's like a parody of a parody of a parody wrapped in a blanket of irony and dipped in a vat of shit. You have to see bands at the beginning, before they're a thing. Back when it's just a bunch of friends in a sweaty basement falling all over the place because they don't care.

Fighting hurts (so does hate, PS) but if you insist on getting your ass kicked every day, you NEED to put on a funny shirt. That way, when people see you walk up all battered and bloody, they go, "You're crazy, man" (the way Will Ferrell did in *Old School* when he had that dart in his neck).

If you're not Benicio Del Toro, then fucking swing it the other way and go for "goofy as shit" guy. Odds are the girl you're chasing just broke up with some high-maintenance Benicio-type fucker, and she's looking for a beer-swigging party dude who rents movies, makes beer bongs, and never asks questions.

This is the kind of girl where she skins her knee, and you notice that instead of blood, there's all these weird wires in there because she's a *Blade Runner* perfecto-bot! And then she's all worried you're going to dump her but you're so in love with her you wouldn't even care if she had a dick, so you're like, "Don't worry about it. I wouldn't even care if you had a dick."

1970 was a great time for Quebec. Hippie culture was at its peak, and in October, the French separatists became so powerful they put the entire country into a state of emergency. Even though the instability of that era eventually bankrupted the province, there's still a bunch of fucking idiots who go to the mountain every Sunday and celebrate it. It's called "Les Tam Tams," and it is a strange combination of the early hippies, the Middle Ages, extreme climbing, and the circus.

For example, it's not unusual to see someone wearing a court-jester hat and acting like he *didn't* just get fired from a kid's show for getting wasted and saying "cocksucker."

Then there's the bourgeois dropouts who do so many bags of shrooms they become forest discharge.

Or the 35-year-olds who have been so fucked up for so long they didn't notice the past ten years went by. Hey, Eminem–meets–Larry Clark, you can dye and pierce and even do wheelies on your Ducati with your 20-year-old girlfriend (that got fucked by her dad) on the back, but time forgets no one, and your mother is ashamed of you for a reason.

"'Ey, while all you maudite anglais are in dere all day in your work cubicles, hostie, I am out dere in de real world buying de lamp shades and making de 'art de pantalons' and living de good life, tabernak."

This is something we like to call "only in Quebec." Only in a nation where people have been receiving two decades of free grant money to promote their own culture no matter how lame that culture is could you have this French clown not even kidding.

When you have your look perfectly down, girls tend to chuck it to you so much it can go to your head. The only way to keep yourself in check is to be constantly looking at yourself with your own eyes and saying, "You ain't all that, Lou. You just is."

Wasted chicks are fun to talk to because there's so much truth serum in there, it's almost like the gay scene. Instead of coy clues you have to spend days figuring out, you get straight shit like, "You'rrre a bit too fat and hairrry for me," or "I always wanted to fuck you, but I thought you liked my rrrrroommate."

Fuck, it must be fun to be a girl. Riding around on a bike with no balls. Carrying a pair of soft tits in your shirt. Being all clean all the time. No wonder they experiment in college. No wonder most sex shops can't keep double dongs in stock.

When little boys hear the story of Little Red Riding Hood, we get this weird feeling in the pit of our stomachs. It's a feeling that doesn't really get explained until you're about 19 and *she* walks by, and all of a sudden, you're envisioning a fork and knife in your hand.

Why cling to being sexually attractive when you've pushed out so many beans you look like a bean yourself? Why not just shoot for cute and look like a happy toy you'd stick to your dashboard? Seriously, this is what the DOs is all about—not trying.

Yo, trucker hats ain't wack, motherfucker. It's those teeny, tiny ones you see white boys wearing. Real niggas go back to the old school, when they used to be rizzeally fizzucking hizzuge.

The scary part about the French Canadian medieval scene is, these guys actually get laid. Nobody laughs, nobody minds that grown men are playing a 700-year-old game of cops and robbers (with little boys, no less), and nobody sees their duct-taped swords as ridiculous penis symbols. It's like a mummy-boy dictatorship up there.

The only thing worse than listening to the baby boomers talk about how they stopped a war and how Jimi played a mean guitar and yadda yadda yadda, is watching French Canadians sit there bug-eyed going, "No way! Dat sounds h-amazing man! I want to be like dat too!"

And you thought seeing girls take off their shoes on the dancefloor was bad. How about hopping around to bongos in the mid-afternoon sun like gay parents trying to embarrass their kids?

And what is with all this praying to the fucking sun gods? If you really want to go back to the salad days of the Aztecs, why don't you sacrifice a 12-year-old virgin by throwing her on some sharp rocks and eating her?

Just when we were about to lose all faith in humanity, this Zurich-looking motherfucker came up to us and said, "Hey guys, why so blue?" When we shrugged our shoulders and pointed to all the hippies around us, he just smiled and said, "I understand. Here, I made this. It's called the euthanasia stick. Kill me."

A lot of baby monkeys can be total fucking pussies. That's why it was so rad to see "Howler" here just fuckin' givin' 'er despite being a mere two weeks old. He even puked! Talk about born to party.

OK gays, here's the challenge. Please find her gross starting right now. Put those boobs in your hands and say, "Eeew." Now, we realize staring at a splayed pussy may be a bit freaky, shit, even we get a bit weirded out by "Sammy with his eye out," but if it was a dimly lit room and all you had to do was put it in (without looking) and bury your face in those suckers? COME ON! Your pants are on fire if you don't admit you'd be into it.

Speaking of 'MOs, you know those Christian things where they make gay dudes become straight? (And then the guy marries a lesbian trying to do the same thing—how funny are those couples?) Well we're starting an organization that converts straights into gays. What we do is we get the gay guy into bed with this chick and then, when nobody's looking, we jizz on his back. I don't know why but it's fucking funny.

Yeah, seeing a little girl on a horse is only "pretty cute" but what about the part where her and her other five-year-old buddies were fucking WHIPPING around the place like they'd been shot out of a cannon. It was one of those things where you only notice you screamed, "Holy Shit!" about a minute after it comes out of your mouth.

One way to get a really hot chick is to show her a picture of your bag and say, "This could be yours." At first, they may act uninterested but if it's well groomed and you used body make-up for the shot she won't be able to resist. Women LOVE bags.

Holy shit is that ever a sweet ass. Jesus Christ. If I was that bus I'd ask him to hang over the back a little bit and just ream me. It would be like a mouse doing an elephant but it would still feel amazing.

Why do they do that? Why would you sit there with a brush maniacally brushing your hair until it looks like the worst white hairdo there is? Why don't you wear one of those stupid scrunched-up cowboy hats while you're at it?

Why do people fuck around with boring wastes of time like collagen injections? If you want full, sensuous lips, just keep calling the bouncers "pieces of shit" until they take you into the freight elevator and fix you up for free. Sometimes they'll even throw in a dental tune-up where they bend your teeth so hard your gold fronts stay tight forever.

This is the kind of stylish art chick you get when you are a hilarious millionaire that spends most of his time on his 200-foot yacht outside of Monaco (that's where the lowest tax bracket is). Someone should tell that to the ex-junkie, video-directing Londonite that's filling her face with bad-breath stories about people he doesn't even know.

You can shit on Britain all you want, but you're talking about a people that have spent entire generations sitting in bars. That's centuries of wearing comfortable clothes, having interesting conversations, making funny jokes, being amusing, and fighting blind drunk on your behalf. They're like friend samurais.

Why do drag queens always want to look like some junkie combination of Jerry Hall and Sharon Stone? If I were a girl, I'd want to look like this. A party-rescuing best pal who can make waiting in line at the bank seem like an after-hours at Owen Wilson's house.

Can you fucking believe that most New York Karaoke rooms now have "Punk Rock Girl" by The Dead Milkmen? What's next Andrew WK? (Too late buddy, they got that too!)

How can racists hate ALL black dudes? I mean, I understand those assholes in cornrows riding around New York on motorized scooters, but what about all those working-class old guys who give you great advice and can repair everything from your clock radio to the rack-and-pin-ion steering on a tractor? You can almost hear the KKK going, "All right, all right, fuck. We'll give you those guys."

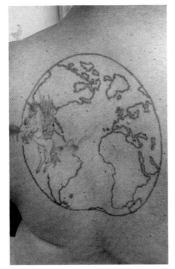

I think this back piece means "When the world's getting you down, do coke," because the pegacorn is standing on Bolivia.

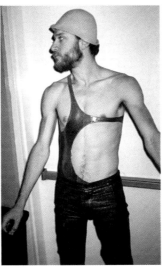

When he looks in the mirror he sees "avant-garde fashion with a dash of accessibility" but we see "Vincent Gallo if he did so much special-K he became a dyslexic ballerina that keeps checking hollow trees to see if a Hobbit disco is going down."

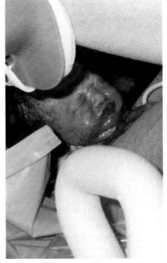

Stop your bitching, you little purple-faced homo. You look like a Russian politician who's been holding his breath all day, and the last thing we want to hear right now is your faggoty little-girl screams. JUST WIPE OFF YOUR FACE AND BREATHE! Fuck!

She may be stunning, but what the fuck is she wearing? It's like an L.A. version of electroclash but with a stupid fucking San Francisco cowboy hat on top. Like if Al Jourgensen was doing progressive-house tracks with Fischerspooner.

"Oh, I'm walkin' down the street just a-playin' this banjo / And I went from Minnesoty to the Gulf of Mexico / I like Napalm Death and I really love to squat / And I'm feelin' kind of punky even though I'd rather not."
-Beverly Hillbillies

Maybe it's time Bravo put out a show called *Straight Eye for the Queer Guy*. First thing we're going to do is wash your fucking face. Makeup is for girls, and it even looks stupid on them. Now, grow some hair, get a gut, stop knowing about shoes, and say "Who gives a shit?" more often. Oh yeah, and stop reading *these* fucking things.

What a fucking treat. What are those called, "pull me down" shorts? And the sockless Wallabes. Way to prove that girls are better than boys. Your feet don't sweat. You don't poo. She's even got kind of a native vibe.

This fat-ass just gets worse and worse the farther down you go. Living Color dreads are trumped by one of those shoulder-holster wallets, which is then trumped by the most plasticky red snakeskin pants this heat wave's ever seen and then fat lesbian Fluevogian funk boots kick us in the teeth when we get to the bottom. Does he hate eyes?

"Oh, I come to New York City for full hip hop experience. I am B-Girl-san and I, uh, do the blakedance 'tiruh blake of dawnuh.'"
Um, American B-Girling is about getting pregnant at 17 and watching TV all day. I would stick to the luxury flat in Osaka where you were DJing fashion shows and getting massaged by surfers.

Just so we're all on the same page here, we've got a thinning gelled perm, lip rings, a wood choker, a huge Asian neck tattoo, and skate shoes with Christmas-tree studs on the toes. Next time you're sitting at home with your wife and kids thinking, "I could just go out for a thing of milk and never come back," know in your heart that you will be subjecting the rest of us to eternal toddlers like this shithead.

Dear models,
Did you know that you are the laughing-stock of the entire world? While we laugh our asses off, you stand there making your ridiculous sleepover poses, clinging to the hopeless dream that one day you will be allowed to stop paying an extra $1,000 for "new head shots." Ha ha. You even have panties on under your lingerie.

Like seeing men using umbrellas isn't bad enough. Now they're using big fucking pink ones as rain hats so the *waindwops* won't wash the gel out of their hair. I wonder how hard it would be to just yank that umbrella out of his hands and stick it in his spokes.

And the winner is...this chief. Up until he was 29, his mum was his best friend. Then she died of ovarian cancer and now Nigel turns to her dogs Noddy and Big Ears for camaraderie. Don't worry about him, though—he gets to fuck them.

While everyone is crying in their panties about the troops in Iraq, some ballsy Liberians have the courage to support the *real* soldiers. Hello! The Tupac Army is the only way we are ever going to take out Colonel Butt Naked and it's time the UN and the rest of the world woke the fuck up. (google it, I'm serious).

When you have a beautiful round ass you have a beautiful round ass. There's nothing you can do about it so fuck it. Let it shine and add a matching 69 so bitches are forced to think of having it right in their face like a big, beautiful brown moon (yes he would be on top).

Darby Crash once said, "The only ones that mattered are all dead—everyone else is in an imitatative state of a dying animal." Which is why it's so freaky seeing him reincarnated in disenfranchised 16-year-olds all over the world. It's the same kind of weird as those anti-smoking ads that go, "I'm Yul Brynner and I'm dead now."

How New York is this dude? He looks like thirty years of painting trains and block parties and bodegas with tiny bananas for sale. His torso is kind of shaped like Manhattan and his legs look like the two bridges into the south of Brooklyn. The rent around his nipples is probably about $6,500 a month.

You know when you have this weird thing with a girl you work with and you guys are out running errands for the boss and you're talking about sex and, before you can figure out what's going on, you're both fucking like dogs in an alleyway? And then, right after, your legs are shaking and you're both like, "holy shit, what was that?"
She's that.

Some girls think this guy is a creep but I like this guy because he's so wiggerless wireless. All that 70s gold and moustache is so Burt Reynolds Florida that every morning he wakes up with a different girl saying, "When I first met you I thought you were a total creep."

The problem with dressing up as a magical Mad Max cyber-gypsy is, eventually, you have to get on a bus and go buy cigarettes. There's no dry ice filling the room with smoke at the 7-11. Just you and your stupid fucking stupid-ass face.

I hate big-ass hip hop shorts so much I'm willing to stand by these things and take whatever piles of dog shit get flung in my face. Who cares if fags wear them too? It's time to take back the shorts my brothers! THEY BELONG TO US!

While everyone bores the shit out of us with their jeans, Chucks, and black t-shirts (what are they *Hoosiers*?), there are a chosen few that have the courage to inject some real optimism into the scene. They may look like schizophrenics now but, like the guy in the tiny jean shorts told us, "motherfuckers laughed at Noah too."

A Montreal photographer sent this to us as a DON'T because of her shirt but we don't know enough about fashion to know what's wrong with it. All we see is a typical "Filles du Roi" with her beautiful horse-mouth and Métis eyes—fuck. Don't you want to just go on a boat with her?

"Ain't nothing but a comfy cowboy thing. All you businessmen in your fancy briefcases runnin' off to God knows where and God knows why, while I sit here taking it all in to the sounds of my Toby Keith cassette tape. You're all like so many lost cattle but I love you. I really fuckin' do."

The two greatest things about the 80s were Reebok Pumps and those trampolines that your mom jumped on while she watched *Dallas*. When you combine those two things with Adidas pink shorts, you get so bouncy it makes me want to slap your Jew ass.

Girls who break up fancy clothes with a dirty baseball hat and a short parka add about 145 fun points and 56 IQ points to what could be a "boring fashion cow" ensemble. Now we know she has taste AND likes to hang out.

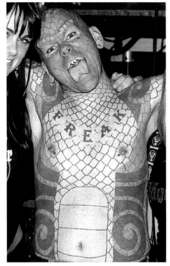

We've always been pro-freak and have featured both Enigma and Katzen in the DOs but fuck it, we give up. Freaks are just too distracting to like. Half the time you're wondering about things like how the ball bearings stay underneath his eyebrows and the other half your wondering who fucked him more, his dad or his uncle.

Ever notice how fashion models dress like fucking idiots? Why is that? Master chefs don't eat plastic bags full of hair. Race car drivers don't drive used condoms. Why do people in the fashion industry dress like electroclash psychobillies that ran away from the forest?

Drag queens don't dress like women. They dress like men dressing up like women. Can you see Chris de Burgh singing "The Lady in Red" to a woman wearing torn fishnets and fucking Tevas? Maybe if the boss at Club Med made the lifeguards put on a hilarious cabaret show. Oh I get it. Drag queens are just trying to make our vacations funnier.

He's just fuckin' throwin in the towel. He's like, "Fuck it. Fuck books, fuck everything. I'm going to watch seven hours of TV a day until all I have to look forward to is the smell of my own farts and fuck you if you got a problem with that."

The picture isn't really doing it justice but this stupid cunt is wearing a fucking spider on her head. I want to be there on the train home when 13 teenagers walk in. They are going to snap on her so hard she'll be wetting the bed for years.

Guy, not only is your girlfriend totally fucking hideous, but she has no tits and her cunt is hairy and long with a pink thing coming out of the tip of it. You can only do anal for so long, shit for brains. Eventually you are going to have to eat that gross bitch's muff.

We told this guy that there's nothing better than a really hairy bush, just so he'd make a face like that.

"It started off as an innocent idea. I'll get me mum some herbal ecstasy to help her deal with her menopause. Next thing I know this lobotomized, Japanese ladybug is following me everywhere asking for a massage. And when I yell, 'get the fuck away from me,' she says 'Now, now, you don't mean that' like she's doing here."

"Here's me and me mates sneaking away from her. Please don't say a word. She is so bloody embarrassing."

Hey look, it's the personification of the problems with diversity. An eye-curdling mish mash of clashing patterns that want to rip each other's guts out. He's not a fucking Bob Marley song about "One Love." He's a junksick Tower of Babel that's so toxic it makes the grass go brown.

Trance is just another word for "E made me stupid and crazy." They love the earth but know nothing about it (like hippies), they believe in outer space bullshit and think they can go to a planet that doesn't hate them (like nerds), and they jerk off in the mirror (like metrosexuals).

This guy almost had a great outfit but he totally fucking blew it. Eleven hand stitched, all seeing, multi-colored, wooly, stryofoam eyeball, necklace beads is *way* too many. He should have had like, three on each side with an iron frying pan in the middle that said, "What?"

And the winner is… a woman who masturbated in the nude until this guy came down from his gazebo stage and yelled, "You fucking bitch you ruined my Glastonbury appearance" while dumping garbage on her. She then used one of the pizza slices from the pile to continue masturbating until she was taken away and put in an ambulance—no joke.

When we drove by this cool little kid and her amazing pink cowboy boots, we said, "Hey, where are you going in those things," and she just shrugged her shoulders. Too bad we didn't have any candy in the car. She would have been cool to hang out with.

Then we drove by this lady and yelled, "Skate and Destroy, Mom!" and she did that "party on" thing with her thumb and pinkie as we drove away.

You know when you play too rough with your little brother and he's crying and he's on his way to tell your dad and you're like, "Hey hey, don't tell Dad, look at me, poo poo, bum bum, etc." and he lets out a reluctant chortle while he rubs his eyes? She's the personification of that moment.

You know an outfit is good when it makes you mad at all other girls for not doing it before. Those shorts make men indignant.

Have you seen those Supreme shirts where they took the skeleton off of those Exploited LPs? This bitch was into that shit before anybody. Nobody can improve on the graphics from that old punk shit. Especially the Crass stuff.

At the end of her application where it says "extra comments" or "skills" she can put: "I can dance in that vogue-y 'strike a pose' way with a bottle of grape juice on my head." And then she'll get the job at WHATTHEFUCK Inc.

What makes this guy even better is that he's British. He's fucking British and his Muppet moustache is totally real. How are you going to compete with that? You can't. Just step aside and let the fucker DANCE!

All you have to do to perfect a cutester thing like this is counterbalance it with something harsh. Like if she worked in a strip club or did a lot of heroin, that would be ideal.

What are you thinking about? How to be *more* hot? Your boots are better than Gram Parsons could ever dream of, and that's only the bottom 9 percent of your outfit. If you're really determined to be more attractive, why don't you become really funny and bear my children? That would be something.

"Veronica, I don't want the fact that I am a baby to stop you from knowing that I am your Father OK? Your Mother and I love you very much and you have to be careful out there. Promise me you won't drink and drive."

Conversely, we have a man so babyish he's forced to grow a handle bar moustache and smoke cigars and get a tattoo that says, "Babies are fucking fag losers and I hate their guts because I am not one at all."

Jesus Christ. Now *that* is a piece! What the fuck is he supposed to do with that thing? It's bigger than Mark Morgan's.

The second you catch yourself slurring it's time to get a water and slow it down. If you're at the point where you're watching to see the piss darken your jumpsuit it's time to make yourself puke.

I saw this guy in Austin, Texas, and he had a huge ballsy swagger like he wasn't dressed as the outer-space guy in a *Bugs Bunny* cartoon. If I had a big enough ass I'd swallow him with it and then shit him out on his mother's lap.

During the war in Iraq a lot of conservatives accused the protesters of being spoiled rotten, uneducated, knee-jerk shit-stains that smell like pee and have no idea what they're talking about. That is totally unfair. You can't be a spoiled brat if you're homeless.

OK, ladies, let's get some basic rules straight here. Nobody's going to make Sarah Silverman wax her hairy asshole every two days, but when your facial hair is getting to the point where you can easily make a goatee, it's time to get out the fucking clippers. Oh, and brown nylons with stripper shoes are another no-no. I don't care how hot your boyfriend is.

Looking at men's toes is one of the worst things about summer. Looking at a dad's toes when he's dressed as a five-year-old girl is slipping into poisonous dart territory.

Couples in L.A. (or South Beach, whatever) are so fucking oblivious. The men spend all their money on hair products and grooming, so, in order to try to keep upping the feminine ante, the women have to become these heavily altered übergirls that look more like transsexuals than chicks. All this "keeping up with the Joneses" of grooming has turned them both into drag queens. Ha ha.

This guy kept whining to us saying, "This better not be a DON'T." Dude, what are you afraid of? You look like a cavity creep's worst nightmare. Why would we make fun of someone that rides around our mouths kicking the living shit out of plaque?

Trannies are gross because they're sexual mutants and everything but then, when you're out partying and they're partying way harder than anyone and they have their fake tits out you're kind of like, "What if I didn't tell a soul?"

Next time you're walking over to a keg grab a plastic cup from the pile and THROW IT AWAY! You don't need that shit. Use a used beer can. It keeps it fresher and cooler and you don't have to worry about spilling when you're playing croquet.

You get a little sneak peak of what you'd be hanging out with if you went to Barbados with her. You could make out in the pool and then she'd wear the white thing to dinner with no shoes.

You know when you match something just right and it's just out of the wash and you feel so good that night you feel like a fucking superhero? That's what Outkast meant by that "so fresh and so clean" thing.

There's even a kind of matching where you have patterns that are so different that even color blind people can see they don't match. That's called post neo matching and it makes bees go crazy.

I know you heard pink was big this spring but guess what. Pink is big every spring. Especially with the men that are man enough to look a little vulnerable.

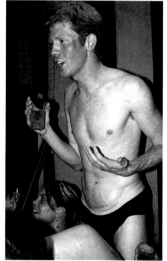

Holy shit am I ever in the mood. Imagine those turgid balls all smushed up against the bar like that. Mmmm. I'd kill to be that bar. Or wait. Imagine it was a glass coffee table and you could lie under it jerking off? Oooooh yeaaaaah.

And they don't even have to be super-buff Puerto Ricans either. No sir. I'll take a pink-faced Irish guy that can't hold his booze and wears the same underwear he wore in junior high. Mmmm, I'd give my right arm to get right back there where it's all threadbare and worn-out.

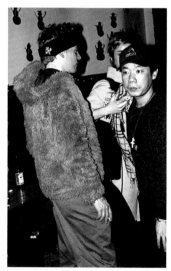

Don't panic. This is not some arrogant hippie frog who is really fucking chuffed with himself for thinking outside of the "pants box"...

...and this is not an equally irritating sissy that dresses like a Russian kindergarten teacher. No. These guys are part of a kick-ass horse costume and they're just taking a break because it gets really hot in there. Right?

Fuck it, people. I am fat and gay and wearing a sweating suit and I could give a shit what the world thinks. That is who I am! Love me or leave me!

Oh my God. What is that thing? She is a fucking monster. That is the kind of thing you hallucinate when you've been lost in the desert for three days. Can I just lay her out on a mirror and snort her? No she's heroin. Can I put her into a syringe?

OK, so it started off that wiggers wanted to have big shirts because it emulated the rappers that needed to carry guns. Then they took on big huge skate shoes (the thickness helps ollies) and surf shorts (the length helps prevent thigh burn) and trucker hats (the netting helps it breathe). Unfortunately, nobody stopped to notice that all these practical ideas, when mixed together, make you look somewhere between an anorexic toddler and Chucky with a peanut head.

Of course, if you wanted to avoid that problem you'd have to fill out all those oversize clothes with body mass. Let's see how that works. "Nope, it's not working out. You look like a giant bean!"
What? I can't hear you!
"A bean! You look like a fucking bean!"

The weird part is this woman let us sit there and take about four pictures of her before distractedly mumbling, "Don't." She was so consumed by *Donkey Kong* that letting her 40-year-old beav hang out like that was totally inconsequential.
Wait, why did that just make me so turned on?

Oh, just in case this isn't making you angry enough, I should mention that this happy-go-lucky Texan had a French accent. That's like John Wayne going to France wearing Marithé + François Girbaud pants, being a rude asshole all night, and then getting drunk on red wine while crying to a thirteen-year-old girl about how nobody understands him.

You know that song by Xzibit where they sample a stewardess going, "Please enjoy your stay, welcome to L.A.?" Well, it's therapeutic to sing it as, "You guys are fucking gay, welcome to L.A.," every time you see some twat playing pool with one hand while he talks on his cell phone.
That way you don't get so much of a headache.

What *are* you? A wedding-cake Fonzie? For fuck's sake, guy, I used to dress like that and pose for my sisters on the kitchen table when I was SIX YEARS OLD!!! At least you got one thing right: You are a badass. Who the fuck is going to be able to fight you when they are laughing so hard they can't breathe?

I saw this human god at a bar in Texas and went up to him to say, "Dude, that shirt is—" but he interrupted me by putting his finger over my lips and going, "Shhhhh." And then he took his finger away and said, "I know," real quiet.

This guy looks so good in his little red V-neck that when he wants you to know he's not lying he puts his hand on himself and swears it's true because he's even better than the Bible. I've even seen people swear on a stack of him.

One of the best ways to pull off a good look is to look really nonchalant, like you just don't give a shit. You don't have to drift into a fucking heroin coma, but yeah, having a "whatever" face is always good.

She's either a half-breed or an Inuit or something. Both those things are better than you and I for a myriad of reasons. Even if that's not an accepted fact, you could show this to anthropologists and they'd be like, "Oh shit. You're right."

Doesn't this guy make you think of the Buzzcocks? He's like the personfication of that song, "What Do I Get?" I also imagine him zipping around in fast motion like the chases on *Benny Hill*. Look at him fucking scoot.

Sometimes when you go out in a real "outfit" outfit that matches like crazy and even has a strange accoutrement like a dog, you can get physically exhausted. Like you're emanating so much vibe it's usurping your personal strength. That's why this guy is a fucking triathlete.

Just when you're sitting there thinking, "Where the fuck did French Canadians hear that wearing huge women's earrings is acceptable?" his Mom pops out of the crowd and is like, "Quoi? Aaah une photo!" and jumps in there with her fucking biker shorts on. And then you're like "Oh."

This is the same kind of thing as the dog guy from a few pages ago. If you don't dig the profundity of this, then go ahead, wear glasses like this for more than an hour, and then get back to me. Tiring, eh?

It's always good to be practicing your pussy-eating skills. Especially when you're talking to a hot girl and you may get her home before the evening is over. You could be a little more discreet, but whatevs.

This guy is like part Isaac Hayes, part Bill Cosby, and part Last Poets, but with some Muslim scholars and billionaire piano-players thrown in for good measure. I'm going to call him next time I have a hang-over-induced panic attack. I'll be all, "I'm so fucking freaked out. I even feel like the pigeons are trying to kill me," and he'll be all, "Don't worry about it, man. Birds are boring."

Whoa! Maybe Miami isn't so bad after all. I know a lot of them hirsute university girls wouldn't agree with me on this, but humana-humana! I'd like to set a trap for this one. Like putting a giant cracker on the road, and when she walks over it, SLAMMING her with a huge piece of cheese. Then eating the whole thing.

This was at this millionaire's house party that had Andrew W.K. playing in the garage, Nelly playing in the living room, and Z-Trip DJing upstairs. Everyone had these piggish Hugo Boss suits or Academy Awards-type dresses, and then there was this treasure in a jokey hat and jean jacket. She'd burp in your face if it took her fancy.

Sorry, Television. British punk was way more fun than American punk. You had Poly Styrene in her crazy plastic outfits and Anti-Nowhere League with that "Woman" song where he starts out loving her and then they get married and he hates her like in "Paradise by the Dashboard Light." It was smarter and more fun and didn't talk about not-fucking and other boring Minor Threat stuff.

Actually, fuck it. Fuck Miami and the stupid European assholes who live there. His pants are so thin, they can't even hold a wallet. They're fucking pajamas, dude. We can see your dick.

"Hey nigger! Wanna date? Hey! What's the matter? I thought you liked white women. What's the matter? You can't handle it? I'm too much for you? Hey! I'm talking to you! You want this or not? Hey? Hell-oooo!"

This is a very hungry, homeless, stupid person promoting the merits of America, baseball, Christianity, pizza, peace, and marijuana. Either those things are bad when mixed together, or they are each bad things in and of themselves. Whatever it is, I don't like them anymore.

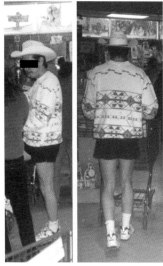

One of our trusty DON'Ts commandos tracked, hunted, and captured this guy outside of L.A. They wanted me to mention that he shaves his legs. I wanted to mention that he smells like penis.

There is something unhealthy about martial arts. It provides people with an abnormal feeling of invincibility that ultimately leads to isolation and ostracization and the need to differentiate oneself from—ah ha ha ha, look at his hair!

I know what you're saying. You just said, "Oh shit." Me too. We've got a gold scarf ponytail-holder, a receding dye job, no pants, a woman's winter coat, black leather gloves, and 11 alligator horns. He is Grandma Man gone crazy gay Hollywood.

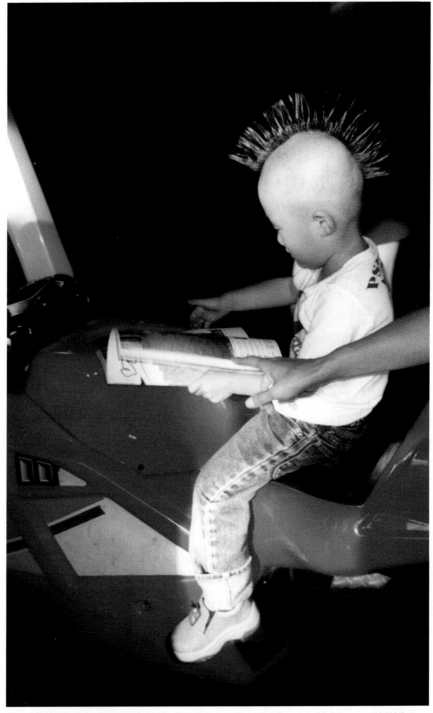

The results for the Cutest Motherfucker in the World just came in and that four-year-old, Japanese punk kid that was in our "Summer Kids" issue (pictured here) is sweeping up every category. It's almost dangerous because girls scream and pinch him so hard it hurts him a bit. Geez.

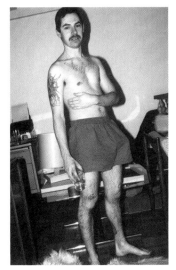

Hey guy, whoa, whoa there. Yes, I would like a coffee but what the fuck is that? That is not bud material. You are drifting into the weird-attempt-at-making-the-friendship-something-more / never-go-back zone.

Okay, first, things were getting so baggy that dudes had to tuck their shirts into the back of their pants so you couldn't see their Calvin Klein ass. Now we've gone way beyond that, and the entire ass crack is in our face. What is happening to hip hop?

It's rare we have simply a "bad outfit" in the DON'Ts. Usually there's some social commentary or some point, but not this time. This is just a really shitty-looking guy who made a bunch of fucked-up choices about what to wear today.

Toronto is the only place on earth where you can have 32-year-old women dressing like 12-year-olds from 1992. You'll have heads of marketing at huge music companies with blue pigtails and platform Skechers. There's no joke here. I'm just telling you.

The same way British bands like the Damned read about American punk and made music based on what they imagined it to sound like, this Coney Island headcase heard about Toronto women and is making her own version.

You know those fucked-up hard candies old ladies are always trying to give you? This is what those candies would look like if they were a person.

You kind of get the feeling her roommates try to find something wrong with her and relish the few times she gets a zit or something. They secretly hate her for being so perfect.

I know I keep saying this and it doesn't impress booze advertisers when we put kids in the magazine but fuck that looks fun. That's more than playing. Motherfucker *IS* Spiderman.

The Angels seem to be going through a bit of a hip slump these days (probably the hats) but I like those fucking guys. They have balls and they do stuff. Fuck hip. I know tons of cool people and none of them get laid.

I don't know this girl but she looks like she might be nuts. What's better than crazy chicks, eh? The drama. The sex. The all night drinking and fights. It's a good look too because it filters out all the pussy guys.

Is it just me or do you guys see grim reaper tattoos not as a mark of The Beast but as a mark of the Good Guy? They're usually older and British and been to jail and they're just like, super noble or something.

From now on anytime anyone says anything remotely bad about New York City you just have to smile and walk away and never talk to that person again. That's the new rule starting with this picture and lasting until forever.

Whoa, Mom. I know they're tasty, but when you walk around the park with a Chocalicious Black Dick Popsicle it makes the rest of us feel really uncomfortable.

I feel sorry for drag queens and trannies. They see some perfect specimen like her and think, "I want to be like that" and then they go try. Good fucking luck pal. You can't go buy this level of catchness. Just let it breeze past you and get over it.

Do you have any idea how lucky it is to see this guy? If you can actually catch him you get to make three wishes but good luck— try to grab him and he just *SCOOTS* out of the way (zoom).

"Anyone who hates children and small dogs can't be all bad" but anyone who puts a Louis Vuitton collar on their small dog kind of redeems it because it throws the whole thing back at us.

This was WAY out of LA in one of those half rural / half suburban housing estate areas where most of us grew up. Remember? Where you came up with a look in your head and then you tried it out and convinced yourself you nailed it? That was kind of endearing.

Proms always make me horny because you know 99% of the people there are going to get laid that night. And we're not talking about a bang in an alleyway. We're talking nice hotel and all fresh and clean—wow.

People always shit on Germans and a lot of the Eurotrash are hard to take, especially on vacation but when were you last there? Dudes in Munich with great record collections and a beautiful cabinet for their stereos. I like those guys.

I am so fucking sorry I have to do this, dude. It breaks my heart, believe me. But you can't wear kilts anymore. I know it's an ancient tradition but the fucking frat boys took it over and now it's all about rape and being a drunk asshole.

Remember that documentary *42 Up* where the guy goes nuts? Britain has a level of loony we can only dream about. When we get a guy in a trenchcoat yelling stuff, they get a guy in Superman pants traveling to museums and encouraging tourists to squeeze his ass.

I don't care how great your hip hop career (in quotations) is going, posing with your dick out for the cover of a magazine is so self-obsessed it's bordering on homoerotic. Go put some cartoon underwear on.

Hey lazy ass, am I supposed to lean in there with my change and put it under your nose? I know you think, "Hey, you never know," like when some pathetic asshole slips a taken girl his phone number, but you *do* know. As Bill Hicks said, "We want some value for our bum dollar."

When did hip hop get so *Golden Girls*? My Nana has that exact same outfit and even *she* thinks it's too much. I asked her why she never wears it anymore and she said, "I feel like a pussy in it."

Could you possibly spend more time on yourself please? Could you do some more self portraits and write poems to yourself too please? Jesus fucking Christ, is "you" your hobby?

You have to admire Pakistani white power skinheads because they are totally committed to the cause and have no personal bias in their arguments whatsoever.

Hey, why is everyone so worried about overpopulation? This guy obviously has balls the size of China, so why don't people just go live there? They could chop down his pubes and use them as firewood.

Are those rubber clogs or are they those Birkenstock 14th Century pauper shoes? Whatever they are I want to just fucking ram him with that gigantic swinging log that was in *Rambo*.

Fuck that unflappable egg motherfucker at the front of the book. The Party Daawwwg is where the party's at. Fuggin'… making all the girls laugh and getting shots and shit. HE's the fuckin' guy you're looking for.

The only guys that are into thongs are guys that still think girls don't poo. The rest of us are like, "get your fucking shit rag out of my face lady." Why don't you wear some used tampons as earrings while you're at it?

"What are cheese puffs anyway—transmogrified potatoes?"
I don't know.
"Maybe they're some kind of oxygenated corn starch or something."
Fuck we're old.

I'm not sure how I feel about this. Isn't it kind of racist? A fat utopian (all fat people are optimists) with an overweight unicorn on her back? I'm kind of offended by her but it's on her behalf.

Remember that article we did on the Mexican art punks? One time one of the girls who lived at the gallery got her pussy fingered by a stranger when she was using the payphone. She went inside and got a Caguama bottle (a 40 ounce), chased the guy down the block and smashed it over his head. This girl reminds me of her.

This guy showed up about five hours before the concert and danced like a fucking maniac to every Streets song. He even knew the words. I was watching him from up above thinking to myself, "Please don't be European." I don't know why.

The sweater has an argyle pattern of hand-cut holes that goes all the way down the back, the beads are from Mardi Gras, and the shoes are of the tennis variety. The whole outfit retails for about $50 and all you have to do to make it look expensive is speak in an Icelandic accent.

Wearing bright red earrings when you have red hair is easy. Everyone knows that, but what about the sporty black dress suit with an inside out T-shirt? Is that so obvious? I didn't think so, fuckface! Whoa, are you crying? I'm just fucking around. Take it ease. It's no fun talking to you before your monthly time. I never know what's going to set you off.

In Scotland, miners who refuse to give the gold they find to The Queen (still a fucking law), melt it down and make tons of huge rings.

Here's the sand nigger that comprises 50% of Chromeo. What a fucking band. When they first started out with the talk-box saying things like, "We love you New York City," we were worried nobody else would get it but, after about 15 minutes of arms akimbo and mouths agog, everyone went nuts.

Forget the chain mail vest. This 15th century rogue is wearing a scuba skin water cooler knapsack complete with a suckling feeder tube. He must be going: look at medieval science show thing, go pee, look at medieval science show thing, go pee, look at medieval science show thing etc.

Fuck, that shirt is class. This dude probably gets so much pussy he has to beat it off.

Pink Cons and a purse are pretty hard to pull off. You either have to be a "fuck it I'm a" fag or such a badass ninja you don't give a shit what people think—both are pretty good.

This is how black people should dress. Instead of the hip hop uniform with the Timberlands and the North Face or the faux afro-centric shit with some silly hat, home girl rocks the Rastafarian b-girl with perfect racial superiority.

I keep seeing these petulant Adam Ant fags around town and it's pretty good. Doesn't work when you're 32, but now it's great.

Trust the Mother of the Grand Duchess of Borneo to show up late for her own party and make us all feel like we were in the nude. Will she ever stop!?

In order to effectively rock loud clothes and patterns you have to be out there every night sizing up shit and figuring out what people are doing DOWN TO THE MILLIMETER!

Whenever those modern primitive dudes go home for Thanksgiving, their Dad yells, "Couldn't you have just painted all that stuff on your body?" and the modern primitive guy holds up this picture and says, "What, like this fucking loser?"

You call that a cigar bitch? THIS is a cigar!

What has happened to hip hop? It's gone from "bum rushing the show" to dressing like Formula One cars while checking the Motorola phone for more endorsement deals.

Fuck the Mack Daddies. Where my Mack Dads at? They watch golf on huge fucking TVs and their 19-inch Deck Rear Bag Electric Mower has a four on the floor with a souped-up hemmy.

I'm starting to realize there is a place in society for pussies. We can't all lift steel and fight. We need non-men like this guy to handle the service industry so you know what? He's not such a DON'T. Forget it.

I like asses as much as the next guy, but this is getting me over them the same way smoking a carton of cigarettes gets you over smoking.

Sporty-casual-cute is WAY harder to pull off than sexy-glamour-victim-out-on-the- town. You have to strike the exact right balance of comfort (comfy sneakers) and sexy (tight jeans).

This genius was walking down Sunset Blvd. in a bikini and high heels. If anyone got too excited she would show them a Polaroid of her boyfriend. What is in the coke over there? Bleach?

When you're a little kid you fantasize about being a grown-up, having a Harley, and wearing a big Misfits sticker on your helmet. But then you get over it. This asshole probably has ice cream for dinner and "stays up as late as he wants."

I've been meaning to rag on these elastic slip-on babysitter shoes for a while now. Having *her* present them to us is like getting a blowjob on a bed of angels' hair.

OK, she might be hot but do you really want to fuck someone that dresses like this? Sex is 20 minutes. Hearing her talk about The Black Eyed Peas for three hours is a thousand years.

We hereby pronounce Christians the scariest fucking people in the world. From that part in *The Omen* where it goes "ya way-ya way-keeree-ya way" to these praying children, we are officially putting on our brown pants.

When hippies talk about legalizing pot, they're thinking about harmless stuff like renting movies. What about the guys who make paper-plate medallions of their initials and embroider them with yellow wool? Not so harmless *now*, is it?

Sure, Montreal can have some raging eyesores, but does any other city in the world have the thrift-store power to pull off 80s surf punk? I don't think so.

Have you seen normal people lately? The girls have these weird vanilla streaks in their hair and even 50-year-old balding execs use that really stiff hair gel. It's getting to the point where we have to dress like native American rockabilly Maori punks just to stay ahead of the pack.

Hello there, my little intellectual French homo. What are you, the advice king? Is there any problem you can't solve? If dude lived in LA people would offer him thousands to be their life coach and he'd be like, "Nah." Friend for life.

This is the kind of guy you see on the street and you make a mental note to kind of make that your look a bit but then you try it and your hair looks like a stupid Jew 'fro and you feel like a New Wave silent actor and you say "fuck it" and go back to the old you because only he can pull it off.

Some girls you just know are going to grow up cool. We met her at the Britney Spears concert and can already see this photo on the fridge of her swank LES apartment 20 years from now.

Why couldn't Peaches have been hot like her? That way instead of imagining a big Canadian hairy bush we could fantasize about a hairless peach that smells like rose petals.

As with acid and heroin and weird religious cults, you can't get too heavily involved with the fashion industry or it totally fucks with your head. Christiane over here probably used to be a semi-competent Moroccan Dad. Now he's called *Saffarí*.

You know how when you have a favorite cartoonist like the guy who does *Mickey Rat* or a favorite radio DJ and then you meet them they're a fat nerd with a shitty attitude? This is what you were hoping they'd be like. Why couldn't they have been like this?

Going through the used-clothing bin is more about having vision than finding neat-o clothes. Anyone can pull out a vintage Nike, but it takes A&R skills the size of Clive Davis' balls to see the potential in an outfit like this.

This look is like your best friend's sister that you never really paid any attention to and then you go, "Holy shit, wait — you're funny and cute." Then you see the jacket and hat and you realize you are about to eat out your new best friend.

This is some genius revolutionary dude from the late 60s who made a pirate TV broadcast that exposed all these corrupt senators and then he moved to Panama to start marijuana crops.... Okay, okay, but he looks like a dude like that.

Having someone drive over your naked body on their bike sounds like a really bad time at first, but then you see her coming and you're like, "If I could cover my dick it wouldn't be so bad."

We are so fucking lucky to live in the East Village. This is how girls dress every day. Like, if you told her to hurry up, she'd go, "OK, OK I'm coming" and just grab that crazy silkscreened shirt out of her drawer and ram those boots on and run out the door. Is it like that for you guys?

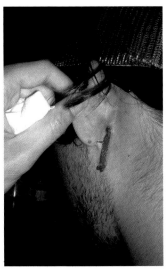

White power! We caught these guys pissing in the garbage and, after they saw our camera, they started prancing around and saying, "We're professional pussy inspectors."

One of the hardest things about first dates is the immense bodily pressure you have to endure holding your farts in. If you don't excuse yourself, you can end up with exploding blood vessels and that's way more embarrassing than the odd poopy sound.

Remember when rap wasn't just a Burger King ad with models in swimsuits dancing around expensive champagne (ooooh...expensive champagne, expensive champagne)? Jermaine, you are a turd dressed up as an embarrassing commercial for lottery tickets.

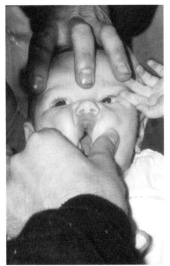

Look at that fat idiot face. He looks like Winston Churchill with a chemical peel. If babies are getting on your nerves just wait 'til the parents walk out of the room and fucking squeeeze as hard as you dare. It's cruel and evil and it feels really good.

This may not look so bad, but keep in mind dude was entertaining kids with a smoke in his mouth and had a catatonic stare that was scaring the shit out of them. He was one of those guys that dogs get weird around.

What!? Hey lady, if you don't have much of an ass maybe you should pad it out a bit with some of those buttock-enhancing undergarments. Shit, why not put on 37 pairs at once? That way, when I look at you and laugh my fucking ass off, you can just give me one of yours.

Women like men with powerful legs because men need powerful legs to give women a good rogering. Men don't have to like that (big muscular legs are gross) because women don't really have to do anything but lie there. That means men don't have to worry about function and can relax and enjoy a pair of these suckers.
P.S. Shout outs to the shorts for letting us see them better.

Guess where this is? That's right, it's in LA. What is it with that place? Is it the education? Do they tell you in school that you should dress like a Japanese raver Scottish toddler goth mountain biker?

Again with that backpack. Moms that dress like two-year-olds are at best crazy and at worst victims of rampant incest. They laugh their heads off at the Sunday funnies as you sit there in horror thinking about mercy killing.

Apparently there has been a huge wave of men having their balls removed. They dress up as 13-year-old girls or homosexual Billy Idols and they are happy as shit. Who knew that testicles were causing so much grief?

We got this couple from two entirely different sources. That's how everywhere our soldiers are, scoping out the entire globe for Biffs and squares that discovered ecstasy at 35 and have replaced mortgage payments with making homemade dreads out of rubber bands.

OK Japan what is going on? He's got fourteen candy red accessories including two ridiculous toy hats. It's rare that dressing up as a little girl is not even the beginning of your fuckedupedness. This guy is gone.

Hey, look! It's an ad for condoms! Next time you think about busting a nut within 100 feet of your girlfriend's vagina, think about this little turd. This piece of human garbage could be eating chips in your house and shitting his pants right next to you if you don't use contraception.

Remember those Samuel Fosso photographs that Janet Jackson stole for "Got Till It's Gone"? How Cubantastic are those? It makes you want to buy cowboy boots and get the fuck out of here.

When you see a chick with a cut like this you know you are dealing with an advanced human being. Instead of spending $700 (yes we know someone who just did that) on some bullshit hairdo, she just put a fucking salad bowl on her head and cut away the excess.

This fucker is starting a whole new thing. Soon these "Willy Wonka punks" are going to be all over New York, drowning German kids in chocolate rivers and getting shit-faced in Loompaland and stuff.

Hey, it's that fucked up Heavy Metal Kid from *The Osbournes*! What is it with that guy? Is he a genuine dirtbag or a world-class scam artist?

If you grew up watching porn in the 70s and 80s there's this weird Pavlovian boner you get from blondes even if you hate them. When they dress like punk rock Dallas Cowboy cheerleaders, however, you basically have to wrestle yourself to the ground.

Whatever happened to that band New Kingdom? Bad-ass biker black dudes that have Misfits albums are so manly their dicks can play pool. P.S. that's his outrageously cool son giving us the finger.

What is the difference between Ghetto Fabulous and dressing up like a fucking clown? Seriously, I really want to know.

And this is just Amanda Lepore in her Sunday grocery outfit. You should see her out on a Friday night where she'll be rocking a tube top, thigh-high boots, and nothing else. She's cartoon hot.

ESPO is out of control too. He DJ'd one of our parties dressed in a Gucci pant suit, rubber boots, and a hat that said "Hot, Horny and Hairless." This is his "renting a movie" outfit.

Maybe I'm a lesbian but how great are chicks who just put any old shirt on and are ready to go in one minute? Assuming the bush is well-kempt that's basically the perfect girl.

What is this chick? She's like an 80s hippie new wave cavewoman or something. Fuck are girls ever better than boys.

Talk about having legs and knowing how to use them. Every time she went over to the bar to get a drink ZZ Top would do circling gestures with their hands and point at her.

She's good too. There's something about a semi-chubby girl who dresses kind of boring and wears thick red lipstick. You just can't stop imagining your cock in her mouth.

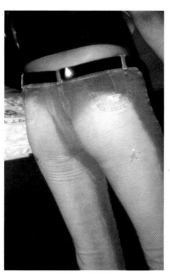

There is NOTHING scarier than a dude who wears silk pirate shirts and antique glasses. Man. They can just go "wchechech" and bare their teeth and you're just like "howe leeeee shit."

What started out as a "stressed denim" look has become something that looks as stupid as when you pissed your pants. Where the fuck is her ass, by the way?

Italian punks are the worst. Not only do they do stupid shit like wear anarchy symbols upside down (even anarchy has too many rules for this dude), but they take what little hair they have and bunch it into a kind of "Lollapalooza hat."

Just before she left the house she looked in the mirror and snapped her fingers and said "Showtime!" but it didn't really work out that way. I would love to put a peanut in her nose.

Ever notice how straight guys are more into how they look than fags? They pluck their eyebrows, shave their chests, and put highlights in their hair. They're basically the new trannies.

Hey, look at his face. That's the way they draw dopey teenagers in *Mad Magazine*. All zitty and spaced out and stupid enough to bring his own sunglasses in to work because they match his uniform.

OK DUDE! I don't know about the guys that are playing soccer with you. Maybe they are blind. Maybe they are so into the sport they don't care who's playing it, but shit, I fucking care. Look at you. You little Rikki-Tikki-Tavi in blue trunks—mon-goosing all over the place like a Julian Lennon video. It's not Nazi Germany, don't get me wrong but COME THE FUCK ON! Can we have a semblance of humanity? Why don't you just put on some harlequin face-paint while you're at it? FUCK!

You know when you really really fucking give 'er? Like when there's screaming and beer flying and all that? Does anyone give a flying fuck what you wear?

French garage-rock dudes are a pleasant opposite to normal dudes. They're so fagét and mild-mannered they should be introduced to all man-hating lesbians as an example of our potential goodness.

Crazy rich kids in casual clothes are the ultimate catch. The sex is amazing, they remain hopelessly devoted forever, and when you introduce them to your mother they'll say something like "YOUR WHOLE LIFE IS A FUCKING LIE!!" totally out of the blue.

Remember in high school when girls would talk about such and such guy being "beautiful"?
I know - it was weird.

Having a fantastic ass that looks like a pair of plump Asian tits is not enough. That's what God gave you, now you have to dress it up a bit. What better way than a Louis Vuitton ass-crown? One that sits all low around the waist like a heavily tilted ass-fedora.

"You know what I like about you, Barbara? You're like me but with a cunt."

How can people be so into trance music? As Bobby Brown put it, "It never seems to amaze me." They're like hippie rave nerds drenched in sweat. They're worse than fucking normal people.

You realize that this guy has to bunch up his hair and hold it over his shoulder every time he takes a shit, right? The tips can even have poo on them.

Hey German mama's boy, you are not in your kitchen writing a novel. You are not at your summer house going out back to get some more milk. You are in our face bumming us out.

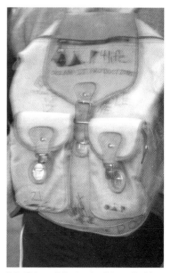

I don't know if I'm turning into my Dad but don't you just want to hit people that write on their bags? It's just so lazy-spoiled-brat that you want to smack the shit out of him and make him wash his face or something.

Instead of just throwing some clothes on why not make a political statement with your outfit. Something like, "Before you villify the Vatican remember they did good things too like end the siege in Panama by giving asylum to that pineapple face Noriega."

You can't just dress up your little brother and think we're going to be dumb enough to run it as a real DON'T (we blacked out the eyes just in case such a douche exists).

This was kind of a shock to us because, minutes before this photo was taken, a Native dude walked by with a Redman jacket that had a huge embroidered minstrel on the back.

Even in the 70s this dude would have been a knob. The Peter Gabriel is blaring. His eyes are closed and he's imagining himself on top of a mountain with his stupid-ass girlfriend on a horse. He's thinking, "One day, man, I swear to God."

Is this guy like, Mr. Anti-fashion or is he a punk guy with liberal parents that give him a huge clothing allowance? Is this what nerds look like now? I thought they looked like metalheads. I'm lost.

It seems to be a rule that whoever wears a "Foxy" shirt looks like a stuffed pig. Whoever wears a "Diva" shirt is as dull as Canadian history, and whoever wears a "Slut" shirt sucks your dick like a fourth-grader.

If you have a wet fart at your girlfriend's house you can't just grab her Saturday-night slacks and go to the opening anyway like it ain't no thang. We know you shit your pants you asshole.

The best way for men to age so gracefully they can still fuck 20-year-olds is to: be incredibly rich, be a tiny bit racist, have an eight ball in some oak box you picked up in Malaysia, enjoy cooking pheasant, know a lot about guns and hunting, slick your hair back, and wear an expensive suit at all times (even Sundays).

Some people accuse this column of just being "Babes & Not Babes" and that we don't really have anything to say about the outfits which is totally unfair. Wow.

Some girls you can just tell are amazing in bed. She's all fancied out in Diesel and Marc Jacobs but you can guess she has a huge tattoo and would blow your fucking mind in the sack.

French Canadian grandmas go so far off the fashion scale they end up on the runways of Soho. Assuming she had enough drugs on her and was buying the champagne all night, that coat could get her like, Vincent Gallo or something.

OK, the skirt is a bit baggy and the boots have clunky heels and end mid-calf (we like either ankle or below the knee), but that warm-up jacket is nice, and wouldn't you just love to whack that ass until your hand falls off?

Back in the 70s, when the economy was booming, you could put on silly pants, glue things together that you found on the beach and you were an artist. Today you're a paranoid schizophrenic who got a lot of money when your Dad died.

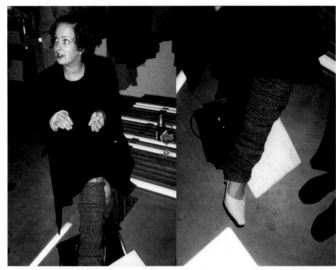

This girl gets the double whammy award. She has the kick-ass leg warmers with heels (of which we love) but then she ups the ante with a great conversation piece; a broken wrist she got for punching out her boyfriend.

Everyone strives for this but so few manage to pull it off. They'll have bad shoes or a rip in their coat or herpes. This guy nailed it dead on though, probably due to those British lips.

What is better than high fashion meets all American Daddy's girl? She's like a High School soccer star, champagneaholic with way too much money to spend and too few cute boys to spend it on.

OK, check it out. This lady was like, 40. Ribbons tied on her boots and homemade visors, and she's a 40-year-old. Crazy has never looked so good.

Now we know what Outkast were talking about when they said "so fresh and so clean." You almost have to be a virgin to rock a matching pink belt and tie, but he's probably not. He probably gets a bananas amount of blow jobs.

Normal people just keep getting weirder and weirder to me. Sure the guys are hairy, obtuse mama's boys that read sports, piss on the lid and dance with an overbite, but the women are just as shitty. She doesn't even know what a fucking butt plug is.

Okay, so we've got the kitten dyed red and the bone through the intricately groomed dreads. All we're going to need now is for you to beat your kids and poo your bed a lot and you're complete.

When you were four your dad was this age. Your dad, in the mirror with his Manic Panic hair dye, twisting the dreads and going to the gym. He is the same age as the Father who said, "You got it, buster!" when you asked if you were still grounded.

We're not saying all six foot tall, black dudes have to rock Raiders jackets and gold fronts but you don't have to get your clothes from Toys R Us either. Who are you trying to seduce? Babies?

Hi guy who thinks he's going to be a model. Todd, you don't have to spend $500 on head shots because we got you right here buddy. PS you're ugly *and* stupid and we hate you - nice headband.

Waiting in a huge line-up to go piss is for people with low IQs; people with no sense of style. Going outside and dipping your dink in the garbage while pretending to look for stuff is pretty good, but NOTHING beats pulling out your schlong and letting it all go into the very bottle you just emptied.

Without the sarongs they're just a bunch of middle-American soccer players that have never been laid. With the sarongs however, they become the faith healers. They are South East Asian, spiritual, tantric-sex travelers that have been to South East Asia a million times (perhaps even in another life).

And then there's Oliver.
"Dear Mum, Don't half miss your bangers and mash but the beach is absolutely smashing. Can't wait to make some new friends - or just muck about."

After getting harassed by one too many rapists, Irene successfully implemented her "reverse psychology t-shirt" plan - ewe.

Remember being five and you'd have a fake leather jacket and mirrored sunglasses and a cardboard guitar? Italians are still into that but not kidding.

Dude's shorts are so tight and small they are tighter than panties. His package is probably melting together like Crayons in the back of a car.

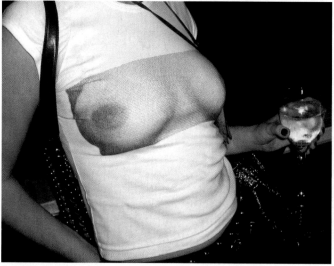

Remember when Steve Jones was wearing this shirt and he was like, "You dirty old man" and "You fucking tosser" to that talk show host? Every time you see that you think "I'm going to make a shirt like that."

White heels with black socks are weirdly sexy in a way. I don't know what it is but they're even a bit raunchy. Like when you do your "nude imagining" you see her with nothing but those and you're like, "Oh my."

Fuck eBay. Why pay $50 for a tuxedo T-shirt when you can show off your fine arts skills and make one?

One of the problems with our DOs section is that we have way too many New York hipsters. There are a lot of rural Omahans out there that have their own magic so here's a little shout-out to those niggaz.

Look at Snappy over here. She's like a beautiful skinhead woman version of Matt Damon.

You didn't hear about dirtbag fops? It's the new thing in Italy: fancy lads who drink Pabst Blue Ribbon, listen to classical, and smell their balls. We call them "grunge chappies."

Pakistani teens are in a shitty spot. The girls get butryic acid thrown in their faces if they marry a white guy and if the dudes even think about non-Muslim tits they get their dicks stoned to death. That's why infidels like you need to go over to your local 7-11 right now and give this poor bastard a real eyeful. All his dad can do is scream, "This is not the party place for all your painting red of the town! Get down from there, you *nat na fucking portnahey*!" (If you want to piss him off even more tell him his uncle is a donkey. Pakis hate that.)

If all you see is some *Caddyshack* douchebag with an ironic mullet sitting here in the DOs for no reason then you are a blind piece of shit with no eyes. That is an original-edition Fred Perry, which means it is almost half a century old. Who's ironic now, bitch?

Who would win in a fight: an African Scotsman dub scientist who plays cricket on the roof and once ate out Queen Elizabeth...

...or a gay Japanese B-boy from Chile who got a javelin scholarship and once gave birth?

"Neither! Those are both made-up mother-fuckers. That's like saying, who would win in a fight, a classy black guy or a tough gay guy?"

Wrong, you fucking redneck. Look at the pictures next to you!

Can't you almost see his boner coming out of his shorts when he gets home? He's going to get a blowjob wearing just that shirt and those little blue socks. Eeeeew.

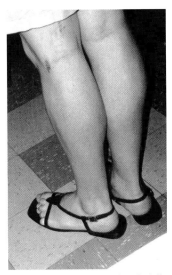

The top half of this guy wasn't so bad. He could have been a plumber. He was talking to two girls about sex and seemed OK but his legs were SHAVED and he had these things on. What are these and why are his toes like that?

You know that game where you yell, "Hey, fuckface!" to see who turns around? This guy got totally freaked out when we did it, because he actually *is* a fuckface.

Am I not getting something? Was there a movie called *Jackie Gleason* and this guy was on the crew or something? It can't just be because he likes "The Great One" and had this done like an adult version of putting Zeppelin on your jean jacket. Can it?

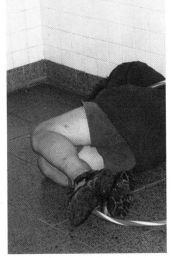

LA is getting really bad. Used to be you could crash with your hula-hoop like, ten feet away and not have to worry about it. Now you have to hold on to that bitch with all your might—all night.

Hey, this is a better exquisite corpse than the racist Mexican drag queen on page 29. They must have laughed their asses off when they unfolded the paper and saw the guy they just drew.

Chicks always rock hats fucking perfectly. Half the time when boys do it we look like we have that disease where you age too fast and you're all wrinkly and small at eight years old and the hat is sort of eating your head. (You see them at Disneyland a lot.)

There's some things that can irk you worse than a missed spot of chalk on a wet chalk board. One of those things is when guys scrunch their shoes to make them into slippers. Maybe an asian grandma could get away with it but a guy?

I don't know why this chief makes me so mad but he does. What is he dutch? Dude has clog shoes on with black socks and he dresses like a children's toy. Stop calling your mother long distance Josef.

Is this some super funny/smart guy like Spike Jonze, purposely making this guy's back hair look like an eagle or is this an actual thing?

OK whoa. I don't care how heavy your flow is you cannot tape a bunch of pads together and call it a super wing. What you have there is called a diaper. If your flow is that bad you might want to try something radical like carrying some in your purse and going to the bathroom occasionally.

Even though they're dressing up for the parade you can still imagine what that hair's like when it's let down. It's metal funk. Could Germans be less cool please?

Students have no idea how conspicuous they are. They come to the big city and live in a dorm and get dreads and Doc Martens and think everything is OK. You shouldn't even wear that in your own home.

Why are people still piercing their tongues and eyebrows? Do they know what is going on in the world? We live on a planet where people like Mortiis permanently turn their faces into trolls and women convert their entire bodies into lightning bolt tiger prints. Everything else is frivolous.

That's a good little stance. Men can't wear shorts that are short because their inner thighs look like the Holocaust. Conversely though, women's upper legs are even sweeter than their bums.

Hey, wait a minute, why does a guy in a bar have a fucking beer coozie? Oh maybe it's because HE BROUGHT IT HIM-SELF! How's that for dedication mother-fuckers? When he leaves the house he goes, "keys, wallet, cell phone, cooz, all right, I'm good."

Some Brazilians come here with their parents and are like, "I am so happy to be in this country. Hello, how are you," whereas some look around and realize, "I am a fucking 10" and rock wooden heels with hip huggers and exposed, brown-skin backs.

I don't know what it is about Snoopy Dogg Dog. You just can't go wrong. Even when he was on TVT and had big hair. Not even an old Puerto Rican dad can lose by rock-ing the Pound. Why is that?

We tend to shit on those old school, Lower East Side, rock 'n roll types but c'mon, this guy kind of has his thing down. You can't really fuck with that. Maybe you're all rap or electro and over it but, like an old cowboy who literally wrangles cattle, you can't really fuck with this dude.

This fuckface weightlifter meathead is standing there like he's Orlando Bloom about to get picked up. No, dude. You are an ugly little rapist wearing a maroon dress, pajamas, and a hat that makes you look like a 13-year-old with cancer.

Just so you know (the photo isn't too clear), these two cats have just been married and the one in front of them (the "driver" in the green robe) is usually holding the reins because the front part hitches up to a fucking dog. Can you imagine if a stoned guy saw this? He'd become mass times the speed of light squared.

Bright colors are good at parties because when you're really shitfaced it's hard to see people and then you see them and you go, "Ohhh heeyyy, derr you like to take baths. Ah'd like it if you wer in the baaath."

PALY BOY!? Motherfucking Palyboy? How amazing is that? It even has a weird gay vibe. Mark my words. Knock offs are going to become the new designer labels. People are going to be killing for the latest Guci or Loue Vutton within the year.

You should have seen the boots she had on. They were these knee-high, black leather stilettos that made your stomach hurt.

It can get real hot in these summer months and, since a lot of places still have those stupid "no shirt, no shoes, no dice" signs up, you can never really get comfy. Kudos to this dude for making a shirt that is just as cooling as no shirt, thereby tearing the system a new ass.

How fucking Hot Topic / punked out is this guy? Complete with leopard-skin gloves and Sid's "Vive le Rock" T-shirt. When we took this he was walking like a junkie that just got shot with a tranquilizer dart which was also good for a laugh.

The gel in the hair is bad and those pussy-ass ear plugs get on my nerves, but how gay is that shirt? So fucking gay.

One thing you should always do before you get a tattoo is lay out the paper on your leg and ask yourself, "Will this holster look exactly like a giant dick hanging down your leg?"

Speaking of "what were you thinking?," this is like the 3,000th time we've had a goth jock, sweaty drunk, wearing a mesh shirt over his four-out-of-ten body. Hey Dale, we all have shitty bodies, but why are you adding extra shading to each butter infested bulge?

When you see little furballs like this you think there must be some country, like maybe Turkey, where hirsute dwarves with attitude are fucking gods. We laugh, but this is the D'Angelo of Beypazari.

A lot of motherfuckers front but to us it's obvious when niggaz is the real deal, killa Queens, old school, hip hop. When fake ass wannabes get up in these bitches' grill it's lights out!

How fucking speechless am I? They're beyond metal rap and Crüe and German biker punks. They are in another galaxy of bad. So bad in fact that hanging out with them would be like E because you'd be smiling the whole time.

Is there anything *VIBE* readers won't buy? Jesus Christ.
You could probably sell them an aborted fetus if it said Krylon on it.

Since when do kids need so much shit? They're supposed to have dirty sweatshirts and scabs and a cheap ghetto blaster duct taped to a BMX. Now they're "born to shop"?

What are you, the fucking Scarecrow? Did Dorothy take you to the Wizard to get you some extensions? You were supposed to get a brain, you fucking world-beat fag.

Hey Broseph, how's your amazing technicolor dreamscarf? Is that like, your one indulgence? "Sure I wear rain pants and work late but there is one area where I just let shit roar!"

No weird shredded shirt or stupid tiny purse, just the bracelets and the hair thing and her favorite T-shirt and that's it. How fucking New York City is that?

Vegetarians in leather jackets are the new angels with dirty faces. It's like they care about the planet and animals and health and everything but they're not pedantic about it.

Oi, here's a bloke that can't be fucked to blag with the same dodgy twats that made your life go "P." This is the type of geez that'll grab a pig's ear and head off to the bog with some fit bird that everyone else fancies getting caned with.

These girls are probably the ones who started that whole stupid beer ad bullshit where you're supposed to have fucked twins. What? Twins don't fuck each other, you idiots. Can you imagine a girl taking home two *male* twins and those little fags 69ing each other all night? Why not? What are you, an incestophobe?

Dudes can be irresistible when they're young and clean and arrogant. Girls can fuck you up when they have that fresh pink skin and something sassy like a tie. Hermaphrodites that do both—shit, they're a million.

There's something real special about looking at a beautiful landscape and seeing a nice lady also looking at a beautiful landscape with a big, beautiful landscape embroidered on her back. Oops, where'd she go? I can't see her anymore.

Check it out. He's got a jacket made of turntables, the other guy's wearing cuddly camouflage, and she has those amazing shoes that are like a hybrid between Chuck Taylors and cowboy boots. The guys don't even have any gel in their hair. Are they from a way better place we don't even know about? Are they from, like, the Maori part of New Zealand?

Oh yeah, I forgot, being a kid fucking ruled — especially during a war. You had your wood gun and your binoculars and all kinds of weird small things made of construction tape and straws. How fun was that?

Sometimes a sprightly little chap can pull off sprightly with such aplomb that you could watch him jump over a tree and you'd be like, "Duh, of course he can do that, he's The Flea."

Similarly, sometimes a girl can get her whole overall package so tight that you get the feeling you could spring her across the room like a rubber band on the end of a ruler.

Graffiti kids tagging bums is a level of marketing genius that people get paid $450,000 a year to think of. It costs a buck, lasts for years and tours the entire city 24 hours a day. Some would argue it's better than tagging a naked drunk chick.

I know you want it to be the lack of textbooks or funding or lazy teachers or something like that but it's not. New York high schools are doing badly because the kids are fucking stupid. Sorry. Look at how they buy shoes. They're idiots.

The only plus side with people in the fashion industry is, after twenty years of saying "I like that sensibility" and "These boots are important," they'll be sitting curled up in the shower saying "Who the fuck am I?" and bawling.

Dude! Your crack is showing right now and it's at its worst. It's hot and there's poo granules mixing with the sweat. What should be the birth of a skid mark is going out into the air and into our world and that is simply not on.

It's the Norwegian white magic sorcerer with a heart of gold. He could put up his pointy hood and kill you with his eyes but he'd rather just light some candles and pass you a joint and be all "Do you like to make party?"

I hereby call bullshit on all monks. Get the fuck out of here. The only thing that you *really* believe in is that you were not getting laid at all and you were really, really bored.

I've said it before and I'll say it again. Babe guys have got to go. Check out their megalomaniacal obsession with accessories. They buy their diaries from Urban Outfitters, love car magazines, watch *Six Feet Under*, never miss a baseball game, and get moody every 28 days. They are faggot wimps, dumb bitches, and douchebag jocks all in one.

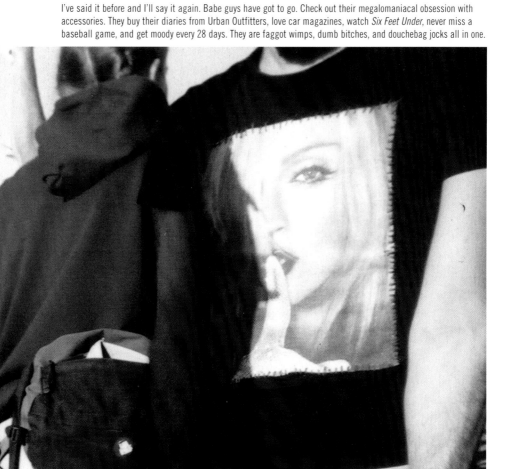

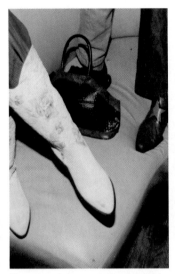

There's something about guys with neck tattoos that makes girls wet. Maybe it's the fact that they have balls enough to makes things weird with their Dad - FOREVER!

The accessories were out of control at this party. This was just one random shot of one table at one moment in time.

And how about VICE photographer James Kendi over here? We knew him as mild-mannered art-museum guy in brown polyester pants and then POW! Monsieur Sex Fantastique.

Katya Casio may not want to do any more interviews with us but check out those pants. That's everything Sigue Sigue Sputnik ever dreamed of.

Can you ever go wrong with a lacy number like this little sucker? It makes everything you do look fancy and delicate.

She's a 17th-century Scottish sergeant / Victorian biker chick / squatter and this is the second time she's in this fucking thing.

What were you, under house arrest? This guy is wearing a Mediterranean Mom's pant suit from the 70s that's soft and silky and has been converted into militant pajamas via a gigantic pile of gay-ass accessories.

With all the brothers killing brothers and the Middle East etc. it's real nice to see a guy out on Sunset Blvd. with peace signs all over his shirt. Just a way of saying "I remember the hippie ideals and now I'm takin' it to anotha level."

And still with the guys and the skirts. They keep trying to make it happen like Sisyphus pushing the boulder up the cliff but no. Somehow it always turns out — asshole.

Someone has to tell American girls and girls from Toronto that drag queens took over boas, Kiss boots and 60s slut kitsch a long time ago.
You basically have a dick right now lady.

Oh easy target is it? Like shooting fish in a barrel? Bull fucking shit. This is not a retard or a fat chick you assholes. This is a homophobic L.A. glam jock fag who's dedicated his life to looking like this.

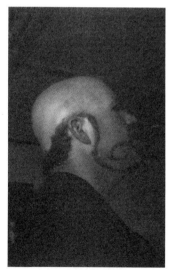

No, you are not hallucinating. Back in the olden days men would see baldness and wrinkles as a sign that it's time to grow up and become an adult. Today, however, these symptoms of aging simply mean a detour for your mohawk and more skin to pierce.

Besides the obvious great things like the perfect moustache, cocked hunting cap, 80s pins, and inside out sweat-shirt, doesn't this guy have a cool face? He looks like Yogi Bear's friend Boo Boo or something. Hey, remember Snagglepuss? That guy was always on.

Hey it's the guys from Impaler!
"What? Where?"
No idiots, you. You're the guys from Impaler.
"Oh yeah, we didn't recognize ourselves because we're dressed up like 11-year-olds on Halloween even though we drive minivans."

Dutch metalheads think they're so tough but they play with their hair like Fabio and spend hours and hours putting studs in their coats. That's the exact same as knitting, you realize (they do it in front of the TV).

Unlike chicks, dudes can keep it together no matter when they last got laid. That's just how they do. They always got game and they always got goin' on because dudes don't need no bitch to tell them what time it is.

Wanted: Bassist with bad ass attitude. Influences include: Walking around town looking like a total dickhead loser asshole.

This may not look like such a big deal but this guy had puke all over his face and all the door man did about it was pull the dude's shirt down over his exposed ass crack.
He was there all day.

Is it just me or do you get the feeling that everyone into speed metal was either beaten by their uncle or molested by their stepdad?

How hot is this bitch? She cuts her Jordaches off so we can see those cool lines girls have at the top of their hips and then she yanks them up her ass with suspenders.
Dude.

Little girl looks are really hard to pull off but when it goes, it goes off like a rocket ship. She's so corn-fed and pure the only thing that could make her better would be some amazing flaw like a burn scar or a lazy eye.

If we had to choose an international DOs representative to send to the United Nations we would play it safe and pick this gentleman. This is literally the perfect vibe.

As usual we have our dirtbag of the month. This time he's sporting the obligatory "fuck you" T-shirt with some kittens and puppies. Why don't normal girls like these kind of guys? Have they ever done it with them?

If a white person wears a studded belt she is a saddie from the suburbs that thinks punk retro is zaney as shit. When a black person does it they catapult themselves into crossover heaven and cannot be criticized, ever. Maybe that shows how segregated we are or whatever but it looks great.

The only thing that dresses worse than a teenager is a middle-aged rich guy. He's got the trophy wife and the Radiohead CD, but most importantly he's got his trademark "hope I die 'fore I get old" leather pants.

Now that getting shitfaced is passé, partying can take place anywhere there's nice chairs, bright lights, and AC. This hotel costs $2.00 per person and sometimes it has blind people playing guitar in it.

I hope dude is for sale because I am buying him to hang out at my house. What a piece of eye candy. He could just be sitting on your couch eating biscuits and drinking tea and you'd think to yourself, The sun is shining.

We've been talking a lot about a "modicum of decorum" in the DOs recently and it gets truer every month. Denim is for the working class and yuppies pretending to be working-class. If you make more than $40k/year, stop fucking around and get some collars.

I guess Nixon was right. Japanese people are better than us. They rock looks none of us could ever dare to try and, besides the rasta thing, always pull it off with class.

We like when girls that were born in the 80s dress like they were born in the 70s. It's so naive they deserve a spanking.

Check it out. Some dude in LA saw the DO on the facing page and decided to try it himself. Not only did he totally fuck it up but he tried to raise the bar by only wearing one shoe. What a twat.

It's kind of ironical that the people who deserve to burst into flames the most actually walk around with flames all over their bodies. Those lame-ass, California, Smash Mouth shirts they wear are rough, but the hats are the worst. Those stay-cool-and-be-warm hats are for Rollerbladers and the kind of guys who fight you for your keys when you're drunk.

A painful divorce has brought this guy from teaching gym and mowing his lawn to some kind of "early Jane's, late Chains, Peppers and Rage" disco dad. I liked it better when they would just get a perm and a jean jacket and sing "Hotel California" all drunk.

When I saw this I didn't laugh or get mad. I was just covered in this sublime blanket of contentedness where Barbara Streisand was singing, "I thought that you'd want what I want sorry, my dear/ And where are the clowns?/ Quick, send in the clowns/ Don't bother, they're already here."

Looks like LeMahn here has been laid one too many times for his own good. He's turned into "Erotic Man" and if you're going to fuck him be prepared for scented oils and Evanescence. He even gets up on his tippy toes when you suck him off.

Our hearts go out to the dirtbags. While all those twats in denim dress shirts are putting shit in their hair and buying sport sandals there are still a few hosers out there that only change their outfit if it stinks.

I wish you could have seen this piece of Eurotrash in person. The top part is a muscle shirt for pre-schoolers and then his shorts take up the other 90% of his body. Guess what else – he's German.

Speaking of Germans this clown is walking around in 125°F heat dressed like it's Stuttgart. We thought it may be hard to convince you he talks to everyone he sees in unintelligible mumbling and bangs on his barstool like a bongo virtuoso for hours, but I think the crocheted rainbow hat lets you know what's going on.

We realize that, as a $250 Samoan Milksnake you are happy to be getting all that attention and free food but can you please, please, please, attack this guy in his face? He is fucking begging for it.

No matter where you vacation there will always be some Piglet walking around in a shirt that's longer than his Speedos like some girl making you coffee after a one-night stand. BTW we were eating break-fast and he kept walking by us with the bottom of his cheeks poking out and zits on his ass. Thanks pal.

It's Dr. Seuss lady! She's got her white leather sock boots and a hat from Mc. Swoots. There's a vest thats so orange it scoots and it floots. She's got so much to matchit by Zum and McRum you can rack your Snootrootler but never guess where she's from. No but seriously –where is she from?

"What a scorcher it is today eh honey? I couldn't imagine wearing more than an extreme sport utility vest, women's flip flops and a skirt."

Too often people are willing to settle for boring accessories like an earring or a kooky belt. What about wearing a mask? Dude is that gay? Fuck Calvin Klein. We say before you leave the house you should put one more thing *on*.

Let's turn this couple into a people farm. We'll pay them to breed and she can teach her daughter to wear cute dresses and he can teach it subtle patriotism. Then, when she's 18 I can take her away and touch her in her area.

Fuck lines. You don't need that much cocaine. There's such a thing as tomorrow you know. Let's just do a few bumps and that's it for the whole night. There we go.

Of course, if you do go overboard there's nothing like sleeping in an ice hotel to stop the pukies. You wake up refreshed and cold and ready to hit the bottle all over again.

Philadelphia license plates should say, "Home of the great friends." Everyone there is so over it you feel like a dick for ever having a problem.

I'm not sure what kind of evildoers this Puerto Rican superhero is fighting against. I can only guess it involves the bastards who cancelled *Days of Our Lives* and bodegas that won't sell Bud Light after 4:00 AM (the rogues!).

Why can't DOs get together the way DON'Ts can? While people in MC Hammer pants and Tevas are breeding like rats, DOs just sit there, too cool to talk to each other. Fuck her dude. Make fashionable babies.

Women on bikes are always fresh but this nice Jessica Lange in the 50s thing is so tranquil and kind it's like a massage.

Not until you dive into punk whole hog do you realize how laid you get. It's a pain in the ass getting your hair ready every morning but every rich girl in school wants to punish her parents by letting you punish her ass. That flag has never been more literal.

Talk about anarchy. Wool spats — now there is some rule breaking. How did you get to be so jaunty? What are you, from Iceland?

As Stork from *Animal House* showed us, there is something about a Chuck Taylor toe with a short suit that perfectly accentuates the sarcasm of the wearer. It gets to be too much on prom night with the "red cons and a tux" thing, but in situations like this it's perfect.

"I'm into Goofy because Goofy was always like, 'Yo, what up with this shit?' Even to Mickey Mouse, who was basically that motherfucker's boss."

Nice. No matter how much of a crackhead whore you are can we not at least brush the shit stained panties to the edge of the road. People's shoes get caught on these. (I'd lick them for $1000 though.)

Why don't you spend a few more hours making your hair into a hard sculpture? (It hurts when he puts on his bicycle helmet.)

"I love *this* logo. This is my 'team.' Players change every year and half of them aren't even from the same country as me, but this is my logo no matter what."
Sports fans are basically just graphic design groupies.

Just so we're all on the same page here, this Vancouver artisan has painted (grown man by the way), has painted (hand painted) lightning, mountains and a whale on his back. A *whale*.

It's nice to give the color chart a blast of pink puma but not when you are Francing your ass off in dark browns and tights. That's as jarring as when you're stretching out a yawn and someone jabs you in the sides.

Ever been in a situation where a guy shows you a picture like this of his Mom when she was 20 and you go, "your Mom was a fucking babe" and then you end up jerking off about her and then things are weird?

Kids are pieces of shit (given) but how about when their parents use them as Chia Pets? You can almost feel the scissors in your hand when you look at his fucking hair. Jesus.

After a hard day on the road Kenny G likes to put on his Stevie Nicks pajamas and just glide down the street shooting the shit. It's so much less niggery than being on tour.

We know it's just a cheesy hippie but isn't there something princely about his demeanor? Like he regales her with stories of his father's kingdom while Zamfir dances in and out of his path. He has a sword.

I guess you're not enough of a wimp with your big, stupid overalls. You had to emasculate yourself just a bit more by sipping Sprite through a straw like your mommy bought it for you.

Forty-year-old guy was so bored in geography class he had the time to draw stripes on his fake Converses and make them look like prison shoes. He couldn't have had any homework either because he sewed flannel hems onto his short-shorts when he got home.

Enough with the old industrial punk guys like big fat GG Allins with no hair. All that leather and hate is for junkie teenagers, not sound techs who carry Stephen King books in their Jansport knapsacks.

Not only are they best friends but they make their own clothes and they drink Blue Ribbon and dance to every song. I don't know if I want to fuck them or be them.

Finally, the good guys are taking some tips from the bad guys and rocking that fascist, utilitarian tidiness thing.

It's not often that a big hairdo tells everyone in the world you have your shit together and you're really witty. The sneakers and denim give her shrewd magnetism a real zing like she could make fun of you and then jump over the garbage.

Prison tattoos are nice. Especially when you make it kind of your tag and draw it everywhere. That's like saying "I'm proud of the time I served. I wasn't afraid to do the time and if you're too scared to do the time you're doing the wrong crime."

Dude has a fucking tattoo of the "Beavis and Butthead" episode where Butthead killed a grasshopper and Beavis arrested him. How vacant is that?

Oooh, it's exotic Asian guy. I'm so scared. Asia's so far away and weird and tribal. Can you pull sprinkles out of your pockets and talk to monkeys? Asia's so cool and freaky it's basically in outer space. Please tell us about the Buddhist swastika, it's so ancient and everything.

Who cares if you bombed the Middle East into a frenzy (to cover up a blow job no less) and then left America's borders open for revenge? You play the sax and smoked pot and black people think you look cool in a leather jacket.

As usual Japan is way ahead of the crowd. Wearing signs on your head that point to your head is so 2006 it makes wearing a silver bodysuit and riding a spaceship to work seem passé.

I have a bad feeling we've had her in here before but what are you going to do? When you're on the platform next to Ms. Nice Boot, Layery, Blue Sock, Fake Fur, Brown Tips, With A Serge Jacques Book in Her Purse you can't pretend nothing's going on.

These two should start a band called Wank Fantasy.

That's it. Go all out when you go out. You busted your ass all week and now it's time to rock some color-coordination and fuckin big tits all saucy assed-out.

Aw, look at the tired bunnies. It's hard to read but I think the sign says, "We got out of San Francisco to quit heroin but we ended up hooking up with a new dealer, like, the day we got here and now we're really fucking high, Sorry."

There's something about Greek guys with mesh shirts and crotch rockets that just screams one-sided oral sex. He probably doesn't even have a tongue.

Ravers are an easy target, but the creeping damp thing that British home buyers are so concerned about has got to go. You're all musty and frayed. It looks like you're melting.

Why don't you just put on a T-shirt that says "I'm not getting older I'm getting funkier"? Head-to-toe, headshop, glam guy is so hiding his bald spot he might as well be the drummer of the Red Hot Chilli Peppers.

Dude, you may be the Fonz in Beirut but your dual collar, rolled up sleeves and reflective chest logo powers don't work here. Watch *Bottle Rocket* or something and try rocking a bit more of that.

Did a 13-year-old girl spill a big glass of bad ideas all over you? I think it's time to cram your flowery headband, red sunglasses and terrible dog into that homo Guatemalan bag and just whip the whole package into the East River.

Remember that part in *Animal House* where the Playboy Bunny falls through the window of that boy's room and he goes, "Thanks, God?" That's what it was like combing the city for three hours yesterday trying to find a DO and then running into this. What is she— a drawing!?

Then there's when you get to that point where you don't give a fuck and you wear exactly what you want, whenever you want. Like a coked-out rock star or some old guy who got to go back in time and do it all over again.

When you're this hot and rock 'n rolly even being cold looks good. Like you're Iggy Pop going out for a fix and it's all cold out but you don't have a jacket.

Either that kid drinks Budweiser or the Dad has trained his kid to hold his beer. Either of those things are so great that it makes me want to throw away all my condoms.

This DO is a composite of every ten years since 1926 (that's an accoutrement from: 1926, 1936, 1946, 1956, 1966, 1976, 1986, 1996, and even one from the future, 19-2006).

She's got that Wendy O. Williams thing. That knowing-she's-hot-but-not-caring / blowing-up-a-school-bus-now kind of a thing.

Mental illness isn't always about self-hatred and paranoia. Sometimes it involves being an interplanetary freedom fighter sent to earth to protect innocent civilians from a time-travelling soul robber. Sometimes it's fun.

After some Ovaltine and fruitcake he said, "Of course I miss Berlin. I vould be lying if I pretended American conformity didn't disapoint me. Vis their Nike this and their Hilfiger that. Zey are like ze sheep."

Ooh you are so ugly and Caucasian. Your silver shirt and your bitter little red hair say two very clear things about your future. Fat. Chick.

What is with everyone in LA wearing wool hats? They even do it indoors. Aren't you boiling? Do they do that just to straighten their hair in a hathead kind of way? Fuck. Now I know how grown ups feel when they look at teenagers.

If we were more passive and weak we would say something like "Stevie Wonder was blind what's your excuse?" Instead we are going to run up behind you and rip those piggish braids right out of your stupid teenage head. No jury in the world would dare convict us.

This reminds me of a good game where you point to some "pigeon-postured, nice boy in a Pop Tarts ad with a wispy little beard and a water bottle" and say to your friend "that's you." It's based on that game "that's your girlfriend" but it's even more fun.

Fuck racial stereotypes m'man. If you are hungry for some juicy melons, buy as many as you want and eat them without shame. Don't let those liberal white-boy academics tell you what your food means.

OK, he may not be the biggest DO in the world... his hair looks like Caligula and my Nana bought his sweater, but c'mon. The guy invented punk rock, ran for mayor of London a quarter of a century later, and he's been surrounded by total babes the whole fucking time.

When your girl has an ass from outerspace and wears leather boots to bed you need to grab on to her jacket as hard as you can 24 hours a day. Especially if you dress like a baby.

Oh my god. Punch me in the face with your ass why don't you? Haul off and lay me out with those two perfect fucking POW! POW!s of an ass. Like we need the red piping to drive the blows even farther home. "Gee us a fu'n break can you no?" (that's Scottish).

Out-of-hand, stop-you-dead-in-your-tracks hot girls look great in heels and everything, don't get us wrong, but how about when they go all plain Jane in a thrift store shirt? In a lot of ways that's a lot more because it kind of sneaks up on you.

Some people know they are going to be in the DOs. They just go through their bag thinking "It's about time."

The Murder City Devils suck.

There's something about a man with ornate chin growth that says "don't let me eat your pussy. I'm gross."

Being a male model is fun. You get to work on your book and go to castings and get your name out. They all seem like really great guys that are probably really smart and honest. Let's go hang out with them!

Mulatto guy with homemade, white-guy, *Entertainment Tonight* hair has got to go. In fact, why doesn't he take that 80s blazer and go all the way back to Quebec where he came from (bet you a thousand dollars he's from there).

I like side bums as much as the next guy but when you rope them in like that it just shows everyone how cottage cheesy the whole deal is. We don't need to know that you're a bag of water. Let us find that out when we're too drunk to care.

Does he know he looks like a homeless bike courier cowboy with blonde poo coming out of his head? No he sees a rugged space Texan that can fly. His brain is a comic book.

Here is a DOs first. Two separate DOs scouts submitted this same girl on the same day. First person gets her when she's all hot and bothered after a hard day of trapezing over babeland and then another person gets her when she's all bundled up for a night on the babetown. What are the odds?

Check out that smoothy class. Apparently Jamaica took over Buckingham Palace and they all listen to classical dub and drink tea in red, green and gold mugs. I guess it started with cricket.

I like Vespas. Especially when you UK it up with those pea coats that have the waterproof shoulders. It's like the polar opposite of an aging hipster.

Not only does this man convey the teddy bear elegance of a smart book that you understand, he is shopping with his girl with total Zen patience and interest. That's huge to them. It's better than listening.

You can't hear this, but she chose "Rainy Days" for her karaoke. That with the Chinese shirt. Can you imagine?

Ecko cargos from 1995 are a bit tricky to pull off but the homeless sweatshirt and sandals are taking this to a little town called "my life is fucked."

We forbade this earlier on but these fucking couples keep dressing like life is a big sleepover and a walk around town is the same as a trip downstairs to get ice cream. They leave us no choice: we hereby curse you with cancer.

"So yeah, 'I wanna be a cowboy' to quote Kid Rock but I'm not about to boil my fucking feet off. It's hot out here. I'm perfectly happy to rock the ten gallon snake-skin hat but, in this heat I'm going to need a panty-hose thin, leapord-skin shirt, some short shorts and, of course, my sport sandals."

There's something that happens to girls who don't get laid that much. They get into purple and flames and kooky earrings and go off on this tangent where getting laid becomes less and less likely with every shopping spree.

Okay, so it's too hot to wear shoes but it's not too hot to dress up as Judy Garland in a garbage bag? What are you, a beach bum goth? And don't think I'm not going to barf if you say it's for "medical purposes" (shudder).

When you see a guy like this you kind of get mad at your dad for aging so badly but then it's kind of inspiring, too, because you know that when you're 35 you won't have to walk around the house in piss-stained track pants with black socks and a dress shirt.

When we saw these "looks like I have tattoos" nude body hose on the internet we laughed our asses off and said, "who would buy these?" Then we saw this fucking clown in New Orleans and pointed at her and the way she hides the ends under her sweat band and she was like, "What?"
What do you mean "what?" We were laughing at you before we knew you existed.

This transexual Gino kept staring and staring at me like he really wanted to be made fun of or something. OK, ok old Russian lady at an African disco party, you're in the book.

I know you're uncomfortable when you first walk in but that "drink next to the chin / swirl the swizzle stick and look around" thing is making us uncomfortable.

What is this, *Office Space*? What's with the flair? You've got the skulls and "Ernest Goes to Camp" and fake Vietnam medals ... it's like you're trying to trick yourself into thinking you don't hate your shitty job.

Hey she's wearing the hash dealer's girl-friend uniform. Crystal Gayle hair with a scrunchie on the elbow just in case and then a pack of cigarettes with a lighter and forty bucks inside. I can't even begin to imagine how much bullshit she has on her keychain.

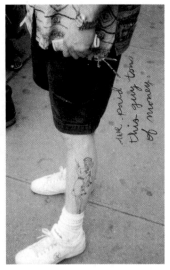

Fuck cramming into the back seat. You don't need to have some fat ass on your lap with your head all in someone's armpit. Quit bitching about who called shotgun first and just jump in the fucking trunk. It's roomy and casual and you can freak yourself out by thinking about how drunk the driver is.

Retro-chick tattoos are neato. Since this guy put it on his leg and threw in the nurse thing we paid him a huge wad of bills and totally forgave the white Reeboks.

That exposed shoulder and bad ass whiskey glare is what "hot mamma" is all about. Even gays have to bow to her lady-ness. They don't get converted (because they're gay, you idiot) but some of them will be like, "I want to have that sass, get me a wig."

Mods in Snipe shoes and Fred Perrys are so old school meets new school you almost understand the Vespa-less nerds gushing over his bike.

Quebec pride is at an all time high and you know what? It looks great. Vive les rouge, d'or et le verte! Vive le Quebec libre!

That's cool - a diapered monkey as a pet. Why don't you just ride around town on a unicorn and dig your spurs into it every time it gets tired? Why don't you put a rainbow in a jar while you're at it?

Look at that collage of green like a big pile of haut couture sea weed. Everything matches so awkwardly and confidently she looks like a younger, sexier version of Carly Simon except underwater.

Ed note: This was in the DOs back in 1999. What the fuck was I thinking? He's a hip hop lumberjack in his pajamas who borrowed his Mother's umbrella. Yeah me, thuggish manboy Broadway hip hop is the shit!

High cut Pumas with tight jeans are like The Sweathogs but with more black people in them. She probably has a fanzine that doesn't suck.

Some girls are such total girls. They have red running shoes from the dictionary under "red running shoes" and they buy great comics and just truck on down the street humming "Greetings to the New Brunette."

70s summer gear is way hotter than make-up and heels and all that stupid g-girl shit. She looks so cozy and clean she's like doing TLC karaoke in an air conditioned bedroom during a heat wave.

There is something magnificent about hot girls with messy hair and comfy clothes. It's like they're walking softly and carrying a big stick. You *know* the package inside there is both easy on the eyes and capable of making you ejaculate across the room.

Sometimes when you're out DON'Ting and you see someone like this you go, "Holy shit, holy shit" all nervous with the camera and then you get it and you're like "YES!"
Check out his dreaded beard.

I am so fucking sick of sweat cargos. What the fuck can that pocket possibly hold - a raisin? If you put even a CD in those suckers they'd drop to his ankles like a stone.

I know this guy doesn't seem so bad but he said "Hyello!" to this 6 out of 10 that was walking down the street and after she ignored him he said "Goddammit, not even the ugly girls are giving me any play these days. What's the matter with me?"

The existence of really old gay guys that are madly in love is kind of hard for us to fathom, so we would appreciate it if you would stay away from the House of Trance and just buy your shit from wherever Burroughs got his shit.

The only person I've ever seen dress like this is a 60-year-old woman in Nantucket. Why don't you go out on the deck with a gin and tonic and call your husband your "night in shining armor" while you're at it?

Is this a new thing we don't know about? Is there a new Progressive Tribal Happy Hardcore Hippie Skater thing that's really huge right now?

I think that when Courtney Love looks in the mirror she doesn't see a tired old crazy hag that only British people can still tolerate. I think she thinks she looks like this: a quirky, cool girl with a great purse that's working on some amazing project that everyone wants to be a part of.

You know when you do so much E you think your dad's head is a birthday present? That's when they figure out you're high, fucker, so chiiiiiiill.

When you try to imagine the girls that would be into this dude's *Clockwork Orange* computer-expert vibe, the mind boggles. Maybe some overweight, 10-year-old burn victims that just got out of jail? Maybe dead chicks? I don't know.

That's a bit rich, isn't it? Everyone knows purple is the color of sexual frustration and pets are the ultimate cure for loneliness. Jesus. Why don't you just ram your diary up my ass?

Again with the male models and themselves. They are all fucking idiots. I hate the way they squint their eyes like they're all tired all the time with their messy hair and those sporty sunglasses. They even like Matchbox 20.

This guy may not seem so bad, but factor in the part where he was bellowing, "Do you know that young girls like Britney Spears will still pretend the penis is in their mouth long after it has been removed!!?" as loud as he possibly could to the entire park.

If you happen to be in the entertainment industry and get free makeup, make the most of it. Use special shading to draw a skinny nose on your wide nose until you look like an extra from *The Lion King* on Broadway.

Austin, Texas, has so many cool, smart, funny chicks covered in tattoos that you end up moving there to be with one of them but then the summer hits and it's so fucking hot your balls are dragging on the ground and you ask her why the fuck didn't she tell you it's literally hotter than hell for 9 months of the year and she starts crying and you realize, this is fucked up. This is like hell. There's even mythical beauties that seduce you to go there. Then you try to run out screaming and everyone laughs like the Hotel California (I just kind of scared myself a little bit).

Falling asleep on the train is relatively safe but with the clever stacking of those dreads and that perfect facial hair, don't be surprised to wake up and feel four wet pussies rubbing up and down your legs in a state of panic.

When did ten-year-old kids get so cool? Look at her breezin' along with a potato in her hand.

Brooklyn can kind of look shitty when you're driving through an industrial part but you don't even know how hot the girls are at these parties and the funny shit they say.

Cruella Devil was hot because she combined being a bad girl with an innate sense of matching style but she was too old and too new wave. This girl looks like a cartoon murderer with vaginal fangs.

Whoa. You probably don't know this but there's this thing that moose hunters get where they see the beast but are too awestruck to shoot it. They just sit there frozen until it walks away. Luckily, Neil Simonton of Byron Bay, Australia, was man enough to aim his camera and catch this buck (possibly the heaviest DON'T in the history of *VICE Magazine*) in mid-stride. "My heart was pounding after I caught him" said Neil in a recent email, "it was a huge adrenaline rush."

Have anarchists always looked this amazing? Jesus Christ, I don't know whether to smash the state or start beating off on to their masked faces.

Yes they did always look this good. The 17th Century was actually the best time for anarchist fashion—back in the burning effigies days when they would kill kings and have big feasts and ride horses with black flags. Fuck they looked cool.

Quebecois girls are not unlike the saucy tarts that King Louis sent here 400 years ago. They're still stunning. They still like to fuck. They'll still kick your ass and they still drink hard liquor with their boots on — sigh.

Even after 40 they still rock the high heels and cleavage. She wasn't part of the riots but we had to take a picture to document how, while English Moms go the way of the track pant, the frogs will be wearing that garter belt all the way to the grave.

Along the lines of the balaclava intimidation factor is the neat looking amazingness of the gas mask. It protects you from tear gas, disguises your face, makes a political statement about pollution, and has this Pink Floyd The Wall thing about it that is just … heavy.

What is it with the no shirts all over town? Is it a big fuck you to all the fat, hairy and female people out there that can't get away with it? Is it a way of saying "I have pecs and abs that are worth checking out"? Maybe it just means "I am a vacant megalomaniac with serious emotional baggage. I am shitty in bed and it would do me some real good to have my face punched in."

You know that Jethro Tull song where they're like "Snot running down his nose, deh neh neh nneh neh neh greasy fingers smearing shabby clothes. Feeling like a dead duck deh neh neh nneh neh neh, spitting out pieces of his broken luck?" I always wondered what they were talking about until now.

What's with thinking being anti-Giuliani is controversial? What else do you hate? Apartheid?

I realize this is cutting a rather large swath out of the population but I hate "guys." With minor size changes they have been dressing the same since 1950. They still like sports. They still reek up the bathroom and they still say things like, "He's the kind of guy that will kick your ass and then buy you a beer," like it's amazing.

Can someone just snap his hair off? The follicles are probably pretty weak from obsessive dying so you could probably turn him into Captain Stubing if you just grabbed a side and popped the whole top off like a beer cap. God that would feel good.

Fuck wearing loose pants. If you've got a good quality bulge, let it show. Why are women the only ones that get to show off their shiznit?

What can you do when you get this many fish in your DON'Ts net? Do you just list the leopard skin gown with fishnets, baggy bondage pants with dog collar and leotard sleeves, homemade Krishna dreads with flourescent ear plugs and suspenders over baggy rain pants, fatso mesh shirt guy with skin tight vinyl pants etc, or do you just say "HOLY SHIT" and laugh your ass off?

Rockers used to drive around in cars and beat up anyone with a C+ or higher. Now it's the opposite. Now Sir Fagsalot over here lies on the ground going, "Hey, I never did anything to you!" while math club kids in thick glasses kick the living shit out of him. 2004 is payback time motherfuckers!

See what I mean? Metal is so Revenge of the Nerds now. They're all straight A students in leather trenchcoats with shorts on that have been worshipped by their little brothers for so long they're starting to believe it.

Either there's a group of girls out there who are into the idea of having their vaginas brutally attacked by fat strangers with Lollapalooza hair, or this shirt is basically a throwing in of the pussy towel that says, "Fuck it. I don't want to get laid anyway."

Hey where'd this guy go? I can see a pair of ski goggles and some fat girl goth boots, but where is the rest of him? Slipknot taught him to be invisible and it's fucking scaring us!

Mmm. It's nice when girls rattle their asses back and forth and they're all done up like how they hoped they would dress when they were kids and thought about how they would dress when they grew up (with lots of colors).

These two are such through-the-roof DOs it's like they're from another planet. Like they've come back to take Dr. Frank-N-Furter back because "his lifestyle's too extree-eeme."
Ed note: this was written back in 2001 before everyone was sick of seeing Pharrell and his trucker hats.

Wearing hot outfits is good. Being naked is always better, but there's a new, even higher level of hot where you're dressed so naked that it's like a movie trailer of what you'd look like nude.

We trained this guy as a DOs & DON'Ts commando and if he's ever at a party where people are wearing flame hats or Tevas or something and he can't leave, he has a cyanide pill.

Low cut shirts are one of the best things about not having huge tits. When you lean forward your chest is all bare and people can see in and then you lean back and it's all secretive and amazing.

In the summer when you've been wearing the same shit every day and it's hot as hell, you feel bad you ever complained about the cold weather, when you could rock leg warmers and cut-off gloves and warm your cockles with a brandy.

He's waiting for a cab to take him back to DON'T headquarters where he sits on a huge throne and has everyone else from the odd numbered pages drop to their knees and pray to him.

The precarious jacket and furry bra top are too much to bear. What are you supposed to do, walk around with ice cubes in your pants? No wonder Afghanistan has all those rules.

Porque los muchachas Puerto Riquenos pueden aparecer completemente caliente y tambien fuerte? Ellas muchachas pudrian caminar todo el ciudad en sneakers y pa talones y ademas aparece tanta femenina ellas pudia visitar los Academy Awards. Es Caliente.

When you can combine a designer bag with vintage clothes you have it made. It's totally "Keep On Truckin'" but without all Robert Crumb's nerdy hate and bad taste.

The jury is still out on what is a better look: cute or sexy. But then there's this whole other, new school of thought where people are saying sometimes you can be so cute it's sexy. Like naked girls in new socks.

After drowning in macho New York teenagers wearing North Face jackets, it's nice to see someone wearing a parka that is ego free. Kind of like Paddington Bear.

The IRA bomber thing is kind of hard to pull off. When boys do it they end up looking like welfare James Joyces. But she did it. She did it so well that ...
"KABOOOOOM!, Aaaah! oh my god, oh my god" (people running everywhere).

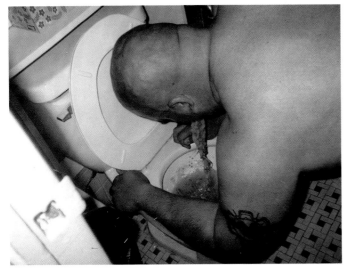

When dudes do about five lines, drink since noon and then do a ton of shots they convince themselves they are going to get laid. They mumble things to her like, "Do you like to take baths?" and "Do you ever take your shirt off?" and "You guys should make out" and they think something's going to happen? Guy, the only thing that's going to happen is this.

Ever since the Trenchcoat Mafia killed all those guys, death metal nerds walk down the street like ginos. Like they get laid all the time and eat babies. We don't care if you go to St. Madness and take witchery, Chris, you're still a lonely masturbator.

When they get back and mummy finds out that: a) they left the house without telling the babysitter and b) they wore her clothes outside. Look out.
Say goodbye to Dress Up for the next two months, young ladies. You are grounded!

I know you think this guy is a gimp and we shouldn't be making fun of him etc, but you're wrong. This guy was watching a fight and he was so fagged out (he was saying, "Oh my, what DO we have here?") that it was contorting his body. Get it? His mannerisms were so fey that it put an arch in his spine.

Look at these meatheads. They are homophobic homosexuals who hate women and talk about fucking women all day. I'd love to just take a carpet knife to one of those Achilles tendons and hear the "SNAP!!!"

I know you were kind of going back and forth on this one and you weren't sure what to think but the guy has a fucking Frankenstein tattoo. That settles it.

Restaurant entertainment is a nightmare because you don't know where to look. You can't look at each other or you'll burst out laughing and you can't look at the performers because, well look at them. She's screaming "sleeping under the STAAAAAAARS" like it's going to get her sanity back and he just shakes his poo dread back and forth going "under the stars, under the stars, oh yeah, under the stars."
What a bunch of fucking LOSERS!

Speaking of poo dreads, it is the best when 14-year-old white kids make their own dreads out of honey and bobby pins and elastic bands. You can tell his hip stepmom helped him with it and now he says hi to black guys when he walks down the street (cringe).

Speaking of bad dreads, this woman has Bo Derek beaded braids that have been dyed purple but you can't see that so you'll have to focus on the loafers with black socks. Check bikiniwithloafersand-blacksocks.com for more on this esoteric fetish.

Speaking of city-feet-on-beach-bodies, how come it's not too hot for hiking boots and Kogal socks but it's too hot to wear a shirt? Check out blairmag.com for more on the confusing similarities between gays and Eurotrash.

What if his father knew that the $60,000 he blew on his son's education amounted to fire juggling on the beaches of Costa Rica with a tick infested hippie girlfreind? Can you imagine the shame?

I don't know if you need heroin to be this slick but it helps. How cuddly is that yellow section of the shirt? She's like the Fonzarelli of blow jobs.

How can you go wrong with some Duffer shoes and comfy pants. Girls can't help but imagine renting movies with you. It's almost a form of rape.

It's weird how all the soccer hooligans now are rocking Burberry. It's not a tough guy pattern. It's a nice old black guy walking down the street pattern. Like this. Why don't they just rock a pipe and slippers while they're at it.

You probably can't see this but her hair has these little blonde-tipped wings. She looks like a soccer pirate super model and you wouldn't be able to get her in a million years so stop bumming out about it.

Not only did this girl look like a wet Mya she was also sort of swaying down the street like she had been fucked all night. Can you fucking believe New York in the summer?

Nobody understands the importance of weird socks anymore. Not since London's Teddy boys. She knows she's going to be home soon and those socks will go from ankle accessory to house shoe.

They don't have video games down in Fraggle Rock so occasionally some of the bigger ones will come up here and blast off a few rounds. It's actually good luck to see them.

Is this guy trying to pick up those 12-year-old girls that are obsessed with horses? Dude, if you really want them to brush your long mane and hold you close why don't you glue a big horn onto your forehead and hang around mountain tops?

Dear Kids,
I hate your tiny little guts. Thanks for making it worse by "Born To Be Wild"ing your self up like that poster in my Guidance Counselor's office.

Speaking of kids, "My kid is so my whole life that I have become him. I read Harry Potter even when I'm alone, collect Pokemon cards and I even dress like the little piece of shit."

Why do people send in pictures of homeless people for DON'Ts. Ha ha he's drunk and starving and can't afford his meds. What a fashion faux pas!

A lot of old Chinese people are really really rich. How'd they get that way? Brainwashing the youth into buying candy and weird bowls and things. Fuck that. It's time to take our money back and then blow their heads off. That's a DO.

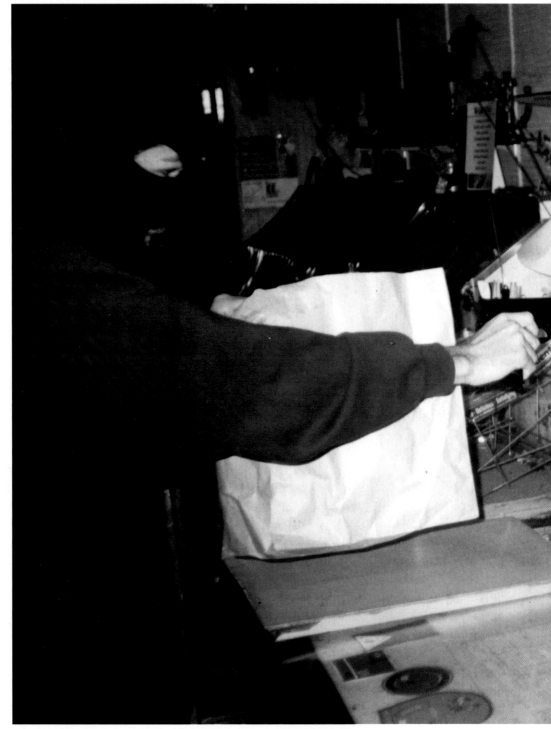

Not only is this month's winner so laid and on the ball he's strutting down the street with a smile on, he's also wearing a Fela Kuti shirt. Have you ever fooled around while listening to Fela Kuti? It's like a ménage à trois. It's intense.

Neneh Cherry over here could give less of a shit if you think she's hot. She's too busy riding around in her shell toes like some kind of British black girl who writes books.

Old lesbians are one of the greatest things around. They're all smart and political without being unfun and, unlike heterosexual moms, they don't have bunions.

What a nice guy spending his Saturday by himself walking around on Xanax. It's almost enough to make you forget that's he's wearing flip flops—almost.

If you're going to be cute why fight it? Paint your toenails the same pink as your dress and go buy candy. Six foot tall girls with big arms can't wear pig tails so who else is going to do it?

There is something really eerie about all those post frat-boy Wall Street dudes with their dockers and side parts. They are all so perfectly matching with that Teddy-Kennedy-drunk-driving-dropped-the-rape-charge vibe it's almost satanic.

The problem with matching whites is that as soon as you get one little stain the whole outfit is ruined. We totally understand you wanting to avoid that, but a garbage bag? What are you, a Puerto Rican couch?

We're no camping experts, but is a garter belt and thong the best outfit for trailblazing? What if you get mosquito bites on your labia? That must fucking kill (I had one on my bag once and almost died of itchiness).

My dad is basically, like, the funnest dad there is in the entire universe. He lets us have beer at Christmas and he listens to The Stones. He even used to smoke pot!

This Japanese trust fund kid has been shopping for dainty wear so carefully and with such elegance, he's turned into the Little Prince. A wispy little prince in silver slippers and hands as soft as silk. Hello soft little lad who may blow away on a gusty day.

If you're not going to go to school and you just want to fuck around all day you might as well get matching bikes and sell pot so you can laugh your head off all the time. Don't be a half ass truant. Go all the way.

Black athlete guy with blue hair gets the DOs because it hasn't been done once since inner-city London circa 1979.

If you get blood cancer you can be a big baby and go die on us or you can fight it for so long you have a cool party trick called "bulging arteries."

Hong Kong millionaires do it right. Like that Shanghai Tang guy who wears silk brocade Mao jackets and permanently changed the universal standard from "Made in China" to "Made by Chinese."

Tight sweatshirts should be replacing bridal gowns as the thing that you should wear to your wedding the most. Add that cozy confidence to the logoless tank and zip-front sliders and you have a woman that could beat you up with her brain.

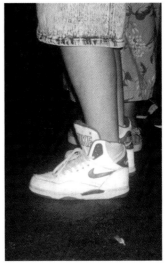

If Quebec ever seperates, DON'Ts may very well become their biggest export. We don't know if this guy is just the most whipped Dad in Canada or a perpetually spoiled brat that had an amazing time in Barbados.

After nerds grow up they often become martial arts guy and go from intelligent discussions about Microsoft to: "the fist is awkward and small. With an elbow punch you are delivering way more surface area to the face which is the only way you're getting the nosebone into the brain."

Nice acid wash jeans and trailer park, Robert Smith boots Mr. Grade School Bully (he's hiding out because he stole Darren's bike).

There is nothing more delicious on a warm California day than glancing through the crowd right into a man's balls. These particlar golden brown cherries are delicately cradled in aqua blue Lycra with a bouquet of black, Mediterranean hair flourishing around them.

After everyone noticed that the Mardi Gras parade is all white people New Orleans' black community were given their own float. They decided to focus on minstrels (entertainment slaves) and Zulu warriors (prehistoric savages) so now the parade is actually more racist.

It's one thing to come from a country that trains dictatorships to kill hundreds of people but to wear a big jacket of the place like it's some sort of a band!? It's America remember, not Scotland.

Cute chicks in striped tube socks and disco denim are so right on you'd be willing to let them cut your hair into retarded-monk-with-AIDs that will take years to grow back. How sweet would it be to have her outfit in a pile next to your bed?

While everyone is trying to get farther and farther into futuristic shoe fashion, a few junkies out there recognize that Chuck Taylor got it right the first time back in 1935. Note how beautifully they compliment a pair of light gray cords.

Texas threads on a tall, dark and handsome man is like a rich and powerful version of tough love. There is a guy who is going to make love to you like a battleship that took ballet lessons.

Some people do summer so right they look like they're immortal and have been pulling it off for a hundred years. She's just walking through that sea of DON'Ts in total control like a Coup De Ville lying at the bottom of a Cracker Jack box.

Shell toes can be a little too wiggery but when rich girls from Connecticut wear them it's so naive it's even a little endearing. Like, she's never had a guy put a finger in her bum during cunnilingus.

Accessorizing is important. Some stop at making sure their socks match their shirt while others are willing to incorporate 10 ft. stuffed animals, hair, lipstick, shoes, pubes and even their own fucking nipples into the overall color scheme.

Oh shit, maybe I am gay. I didn't know it until someone made a dress that looks like a big wet bag of womanness.

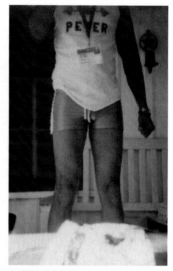

Trucker hats and baseball shirts are corny now but what if you're from Texas and you play professional baseball and drive a truck and could give less of a shit what people in New York think?

He looks like one of those "rules guys" that insists you chug a beer if you fart without saying, "Safety." It can seem irritating at the time but then you realize you laughed your ass off all night and got totally hammered.

As GBV's Bob Pollard is quick to point out, "dick pants are back." If you've got a little extra dick you'd be an idiot not to show it off.

Actually, you know what? Let's push the envelope even farther and squeeze into some baby's underwear. There's some cleavage for you. You little sluts.

If you get a lot of headaches it's good to sort of make it your own and get a tattoo of how it feels, all over your head, forever. That way the headache goes, "Shit" and goes away.

In a town like Austin where everyone does the same thing, it's nice to see some people go their own way and do totally un-Texas things like only have a few tattoos and talk to black people.

High school teachers that want to rent an overhead projector have to go through the Audio Visual (AV) guys. There's always one really fat guy with a beard and one guy that looks like this.

It's hard to see here, but we promise this woman has a candelabra of ejaculating blue penises tattooed on her arm.

You've heard of Boy Scouts, well these Turbonegro fanatics call themselves Man Scouts and they personify that great British adjective nobody ever uses here. He's "wet."

It's fun to ride your motorbike with no helmet but, when you get to the bar, take the extra time to go the bathroom and check what the wind has done to your bangs.

Though the t'aint holds many erotic secrets, that nebulous area between your bag and your anus is not to be photographed. Ever.

Nice hat you fucking pig.

The first time I ever used my time-traveling belt I went to the year 2044 and this dude appeared out of nowhere. "Hello, I am Mr. Crafty," he said, "I will be your guide. Do you have any questions about the belt?"

These are two German gay dudes and the guy on the right wanted to dump the guy on the left weeks ago but they had already bought tickets to come here to New York so he figured he'd just dump him after they got back. It's only a few days right? Wrong! Dude on the right is suffering right now way worse than he ever could have imagined. He is in hellll. The blonde guy subconsciously senses this and is acting really weird and affectionate trying to overcompensate. They are both going to get cancer from the subliminal stress of this trip.

Thank you Quebec. Thank you for taking us back to those days where we had to get out of bed and tell our drunk and stoned parents to turn down the Steely Dan because we had to go to school the next day. They would smoke pot out of weird margarine containers and fall asleep to "Blue Bayou" by Linda Ronstadt.

Self-conscious J.A.P.s with fat asses are permitted to wear shirts around their waists but who let Canadian ginos in on the deal? Dude, you look like the A&W Root Beer Bear on his lunch break.

This crackhead was talking to two Japanese tourists so fast it sounded like lazer tag. Instead of understanding a word he said they just sat there wondering how he managed to fit his pants so far up his anal canal.

X-treme guys are no longer satisfied with riding mountain bikes into trees and jumping off elevators. Now they wear X-treme clothes like floppy fleece raver hats from the 80s, scuba sweaters and, fuck it, a woman's handbag.

When everyone is bitching about the cold it's a DO to take off your clothes and dance on a pile of ice while clowns grapple at your feet wondering what to do.

It looks hot when you dress up as a cartoon, especially when you can pull off that Fantasia thing that makes us think the sex is going to be all mystical and heavy with big magic things flying everywhere.

We love that European "you've never seen this sweater before" kind of super-different thing. All those totally new-looking soccer shoes and little logo-less patches are what makes clothing outside of North America so great. They all look like they're out of a story book called Vernon and Varian Go for a Walk or something.

Wearing all white is rad because nobody else does it. Your shit gets dirty and you get these dark areas where your hands go in your pocket but that's a good thing. Like a British aristocrat who lives in Bangladesh. You're pristine but lived in.

You can think and think and think your ass off trying to come up with a witty slogan for your iron-on T-shirt or you can just think of something that you really like and just say, "fuck it" and get that.

If you're going to have a bunch of girls over for an anal orgy be smart about it and get an enema kit set up first. Sure they'll fuck around with the cord for awhile and goof off but, eventually, they will turn over and do as they're told (I just gave myself a boner).

I saw this guy on the train (there's a bun at the back, too) but didn't have a camera (shit!). Soon after, a stranger came into our office and said, "You want this?" It made me scared to know that God cares about the DON'Ts.

Tight-fitting jean jackets are always a safe bet but to combine the 70s vibe with an outer-spacey, angel thing is so out-of-control babe, it's odd. Like when you're so hot you're more something like a phenomenon than just something sitting there.

OK everyone needs to take it easy on the mandatory water bottle (what is this, the desert?) but everything else is great. Her little red shoes and tiny number six manage to distribute just the right level of cute. Not creepy, "I'm 6 years old" cute but more of a, "Have you heard that song 'Honey' by The Affair?" cute.

LA has either the tackiest people on earth or the best-dressed people on earth. Check out that denim vest, sweatshirt combination. It brings her T-shirt to life like Frankenstein during an electrical thunderstorm.

Most girls think knitted dresses are tacky and would say this girl looks like a bath mat from Pier 1 Imports but at least it's better than when your girlfriend is so excited to go out she cakes her face in clown make up and puts on shoes so excruciating she's complaining all night.

Open backs are like bare chests but legal. Who cares about nipples when you have two baby soft shoulder blades caressed by the occasional cotton strap?

This is the best "two birds with one stone" we ever snapped. We've got Suzanne Somers from the poodle trailer park together with an intensely proud but tumorous, wet-look mullet. The photographer took the day off after this.

I know it's not really a "DON'T" to be a mentally ill fag but could this guy look more like cum? Ew, wipe him off me.

You see a vain wanker with L'Oreal hair and a fetish for his own arms. We see (we know) a nightmare rockstar that plays the tiny guitar like the elves in *Spinal Tap* but forever. Even after his gay band's set is over he'll sit there plucking out tunes to match whatever people are playing on the jukebox.

Hey, go nuts with the patterns. There's nothing wrong with that. But, unless you're a lonely Greek girl visiting Paris for a very short time, don't let patterns get to the point where you are walking down the street with a picture of an Eiffel Tower up our ass.

"Are you going to make me a DON'T just because I did so much acid my mind is a reeking piece of moss full of misguided patriotism and 60s elf worship?"

I fucking love the hard-labor look. Imagine him with that mask hanging around his neck and a Guinness in his hand sitting at the pub after a hard day's work with BTO playing in the background. I think I'm going to simulate that look using baby powder.

What a world it is, when a guy in a thick flannel shirt (held tight against his body with suspenders) can crouch down on his white-corduroyed knees and start necking with a punk stunner. What is this, the Holodeck?

Hey, don't get us wrong. If you want to shave hamsters or put monkeys up your ass or whatever that's cool - whatever gets you up in the morning. But leaving the animal in there with the tail hanging out? That is disgusting.

Either this person is sleepwalking or someone is so comfortable with himself he's decided to go out on the town in his Sunday-at-home clothes. It's all right to be cozy and everything, but you look like you're my friend's dad and you just came upstairs to tell us to turn the music down.

In ballet there's 1st position, 2nd position and the elusive 3rd position, where you push your back into perfect posture and sit with your beer between your legs like an altar boy. It helps to wear a huge open collar like a ballerina because it gets you into the mood.

Here we have a bold fashion statement that says "yeah it's cold out and I'm almost fifty years old but I am going to throw all kinds of purple around and match like fuckin' crazy until I die."

Dressing exactly like your roommate has gone from a nutty idea for a Friday night to a giant sign that says, "We shouldn't have moved to the big city because we are scared shitless."

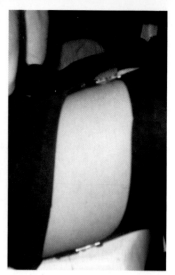

Dressing as a funny rabbit with your hand wailing all over the place and huge ears before busting into showtunes is so good it's like an eye massage. These should be mandatory uniforms for all the parties in all the land.

Check out the attention to detail we have going here. Not only is the matching pitter patter of warm reds a relief from the winter blues, but we've cherried the sundae with a little warm color star patch. It's nobody I would fuck but I'd like my kid brother to be dating her.

Garter belts and other things like that aren't particularly sexy in and of themselves. The turn-on is that someone is so into sex they are willing to complicate their lives with an uncomfortable and cumbersome thing just to attract more lovers. It's like carrying around a 300lb. sign that says "I like to fuck."

The raver knapsacks can go (cut her some slack here this is Quebec) but there's something about legwarmers that makes girls so girly. They're like the best of socks and boots combined.

The paradox of having a coy and gentle girl with bad-ass tattoos is a double whammy punch of nice that either means she is a total prude trying to feign toughness or she is a well educated farm girl that will wear high heels to bed. We're going to assume it's the latter.

The 1980s were a time when Missing Person's Dale Bozzio and 'Til Tuesday's Aimee Mann could dance over to their ex-boyfriends yelling "Lies, Lies, Lies yeah" while all their friends danced in perfect unison for support. Dressing like that now is a way of reminding us how fucking fun that era was.

Hey, asshole! Do you know how irritating all your theories about religion and romance and "this crazy planet we live on" are? I'll tell you: Every time you talk, your wife and kids zone out and have fantasies about your head falling off. You are officially on Schindler's bored shitlist so put on some shoes and get the fuck out of here.

If you ever can't get ahold of me, try calling Ross and Sandy's. I sit at the kitchen table with Sandy and tell her my problems while Ross is getting a beer out of the fridge and saying, "You think too much, man. Just fucking relax. Do you want a beer?" Why hang out anywhere else?

One thing you have to realize about shoes is, at a party, nobody really sees them. That's why it's smart to have a casual cute ensemble at the top and then, fucking, KAPOW! crazy shoes at the bottom. People only see them like, twice, and they remember it for the rest of their lives.

Holy tattoo balls the size of hairy watermelons. He has a fucking jigaboo, minstrel, jungle monkey on his body until he dies. The funniest part is nobody has brought it up or noticed it in the ten years he's had it. I don't know what's more offensive.

Speaking of offensive, I hate pedophiles' gross, disgusting guts (especially "artists") and that is precisely why this T-shirt is so amazing. It made me gasp and I am a <u>vile</u> pig.

Once you settle down with a beer like Bud Light you can stop worrying about your weight and just chillll. Just put on your Mom's nightie, quit your job, eat lots of cheese and just chillll.

The people of Quebec are very proud of the early Middle Ages. Court jestering was generating more income than all of the other provinces combined and the juggling market was thriving. Who can blame this melancholy gentleman, then, for harkening back to those glory days in this daring splash of old fashioned clobber and pointy hat.

Shut up with those fuckin' horns at Quebec's winter Carnival. What are you, a bird? Twaaaaaaaan twaaaaaaank back to some other guy a quarter of a mile away who's going tweeeeeeeerrrre tweeeeeeeeerre.

I hate it when people make their insecurities really obvious. Like when bald guys put sunglasses on their forehead to create a hair-like diversion. It's so transparent it's embarrassing.

OK, Little Miss Racist, let's try to take it easy. Just because your mom's taking two seconds out of your day to talk to a black man does not give you the right to start freaking out and crying like it's 1999. It's the year 2004 young lady. Get with it.

Speaking of racism. Sometimes reality can be so harsh it looks like a KKK cartoon.

Part of dressing punk means you have to be a bit uncomfortable if it's hot out — sorry. If you don't like it become a skater or tennis guy or something. Shorts are not allowed.

Fuck Cuddle Parties, if you really want to "create a safe space for men and women to reinvent play time" you might want to try a fruit drink orgy like this. You get the same affectionate joy but without all the sock touching (I really hope cuddleparty.com is still up when you read this).

In fact, the only thing better than fruit drink orgies is stumbling across a whole bunch of women that order beer by themselves because they think gin and tonics taste gross. We love it in such a homo way it's basically "on the DL."

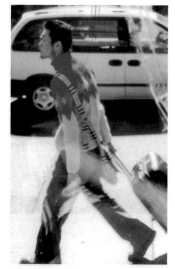

Do you have to have amazing shit to be from Japan? What do they do to you if you look like some of the people on the next page? Seriously, do you just not get laid or do they give you the finger when you walk down the street.

Just when all that Gap camo shit was giving you narcolepsy, this little explosion of color walks on to the scene and gives us a blast of delicious sunshine. Not unlike when you're a kid and you bite into a brand new piece of banana Bubbalicious.
It's tiring for him, though, so don't crowd.

Man, when girls have this black hair and they make it into a Betty Rubble thing instead of making a big deal of it right down their back. It's so domestic and smart it makes you want to own a record store.

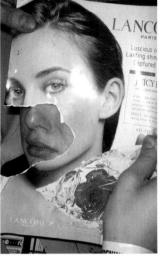

We're not sure what's worse, pulling on a soft dick that has a fucking Prince Albert in it or necking with a trannie just moments after he got his tits put in. They're both from the planet Barf.

What is it with people that just fucking stand there for a living? Nice job you silly cow. You are a professional stander there. What is with the attitude? The only people that are impressed are: lonely people, fat guys, and really, really, rich Greek men that are involved in "import and export."

Working class Canadians like New Mexico sweaters, brown couches that smell like cigarettes and really expensive leather cowboy hats. A lot of them have been forced into that world by classism but a lot of them are just really fucking tacky and stupid.

He insisted on the surgery because he's a "woman trapped in a man's body" but the surgeon misunderstood and created a "man trapped in a woman's body."

French Canadians love the following: Patagonia baby scarves tied at 90°, brightly coloured jeans, women's socks, and wrap around sunglasses. This is what happens when a Mummy's boy gets cold.

I like to have every last centimeter of my shit be some kind of thing. A Travis Bickle lighter, soap that has two animals fucking, a Kleenex box that looks like the car from *Animal House*, shit, even my underwear is some crazy rock shirt thing that a fag made me.

Why did they have to get that geriatric slapper Lori Petty to play Tank Girl? Everyone in Hollywood is so gross and corny compared to us.

Every skate park has some eccentric old guy with a Bud and long hair who talks about the government and blah blah, but how many of them regularly pick up a deck and tear the bowl a new ass? In Pro Design knee pads no less!

Fedoras are really hard to pull off. Most of the time you end up looking like a foppish nerd who wants to solve crimes and perform magic. The only way you can pull it off is to be a stoned, badass nice guy with weird tattoos and something really dangerous to do later on, like this guy.

Fighting always looks great. Girls like it because there's this weird cave thing in the back of their heads where they are like, "He will protect my young."

It's smart to go to a party wearing a shirt that everyone thinks you borrowed from your dad because you puked, but it's really a vintage Polo that you got on eBay for $400.

If you're really partying and doing things like posing with beers a lot, you need a versatile purse to hold your shit in. As Four's circular bags may be incredibly expensive Euro bullshit but they are perfect for holding lots of booze and stolen sandwiches without feeling bogged down.

Ooh I'm so scared, Metal Machine Montrealer. What are you going to do, hit me in the face with your mom?

Pigs are always DON'Ts because it is their job to shit on your party, but when they go on a Work to Rule strike you get to see what twats they really are... what Guess jean/Levi's 501 boot cut wearing twats they really are.

We thought lone rider cool guys went out with the *Bad News Bears*, but no. You still have Marlboro-smoking Fonzes out there who talk with a squint and drive off into the sunset pretending it has nothing to do with the fact that they are TOTAL pussies?

Ugh, what could be worse than that early teen stage where you start experimenting with different colors and you get some lip piercing to match a medallion from the 60s that you found in your mom's old make-up drawer? No wonder fathers hate their sons.

Oh I know what's worse. A broke 42-year-old who's still in that stage. He decorated his paper-thin jogging pants with random swirls of spray paint and his blazer is a color that doesn't even exist. He's dreaming of being on Nickelodeon.

Someone has to tell Afro AmeriDONT's that just because something is expensive and bright, it doesn't mean it's not just a ridiculous tarp with cargo pockets.

Laverne and Shirley meets Japanese Dr. Who. That means: you are fun and work at the beer factory (best friend material) but you're also a heroic fighter.

Leather jackets are hard to pull off especially when you have one of those typical white trash thin ones made out of leather ties. When you get the good ones however, you go from alcoholic carpenter to Guitar Wolf, graphic design guy.

Those shoes are neat. Neat enough to make boys forget that they want you to wear high heels. Then you add her frumpy Grandma don't-give-a-shit thing and she becomes this super shit together woman that doesn't even have a TV.

Oh the snow queen. She's so delicate and fragile in her spotless linens that she can float over to get an espresso and then just blow away in the wind with just a pile of daffodils and doves fluttering around in the area where she just was.

White people's hair has so many varieties it's boring to see it dyed. When you're one of those races that only has black hair however, it's nice to watch. Especially when counter-balanced with a utilitarian anorak.

They may be so hazardous to drive with that car accidents have increased 24% since the trend began but holy shit. It's like *Soul Train* meets Scottish school girls.

We're no fashion experts or anything but we would hazard to guess that dressing up like it's 1985 and doing this weird footlooseflashdance all over the street in the middle of the afternoon might be a bit fucked in the head. Nice leather tie and pointy shoes and nice brown nylons and blue eyeshadow you Crasians.

She has somehow managed to make this furry animal knapsack look so disgusting it might as well be an aborted fetus with a big zipper sewn across its head.

This guy looks like a little elf-troll who got left behind after a Dio concert. One extra special feature that you probably can't see here is the shaved head with a lesbian rat tail of clumpy dreads like it's 1462.

If you're so knock-kneed your legs look like an upside down Y, you might not want to accentuate it with candy striped slut socks. It's like a thalidomide guy wearing a studded wrist band.

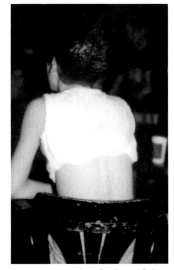

What have we got here. The instant Baby-T? You just roll your whole outfit into a series of donuts whenever you're too hot?

Discharge were good but they got a bit noisy at times. But Crass? Jesus Christ. Have you ever listened to that antichrist poem by Eve Libertine where she's like, "Christy Christus, I puke upon your papal throne." That is some of the heaviest shit in the history of punk rock.

"Aw fuck, Zorf was totally wrong. Earthlings don't dress like geriatric gay Italians."
Will you shut up and just relax. We're fine.

You might see me as an Integrated Aircraft Systems engineer that listens to prog rock and masturbates too much but, inside, lurks a deadly fucking cyber alien monster thing that isn't a nerd one bit.

Ugh, sometimes when people start really churning them out it's truly disgusting. It's like they're possums or something.

Thanks again God – for Tori Amos man. I could probably jerk off to this guy dancing.

How could someone who lives in a well-populated North American city still be working the "flaxen hair" bit? Is he like "I've heard the Fabio jokes but whatever, this is who I am" or does he have no clue?

The good thing about those "somebody, somewhere is sick of her shit" shirts is they help you get on with your life when one of these heavily lip-glossed Soho b-girls walks by. Just pretend she's a moody nightmare and has a cottage cheese ass or something.

Fuck dick pants. They were over pages and pages ago. Now you have "give my ass a good honk" pants and it's right out there.

She's all done out with the shoes by Palta Italy, pants by Paul Hainks and a Dolé shirt or whatever. I made those up but you know it's some super expensive shit.

You can tell when vintage jean jackets are real. There's something about the way they wrinkled back then that just can't be faked.

We went to see Maiden this week and happened upon hundreds of unintentional DOs. They had perfect Harley purses and hot feathered hair and were so far gone into white trash land they had become haute couture.

I smoked crack with this guy (not kidding).

Er, hello? Fuckface? What the shit are you doing? Turn to your right and start talking and talking and talking and keep talking until you're at her house (remember how it goes: talking... laughing... fucking). What is the matter with the kids today? Dude, she looks like a supermodel cartoon where a squirrel or Pepe le Pew or whatever sees a super-hot female version of whatever he is and he gets so excited his eyes pop out of their sockets and go KA-ZOING. Why aren't your eyes popping out of your head you dick!?

A lot of fags will tell you guys look good with jizz on their faces and, if you're in love, that may very well be true. But from a straight perspective, we think nothing looks better than a guy with his face just dripping with hot, wet, beer. And then he's all licking it like a little whore... I'm getting a heteroboner.

The hot new thing in New York right now is androgynous 70s Jesus fags. It's, like, bigger than Studio 54.

And it doesn't matter if it's a guy being a woman or a woman being a guy. EVERY-ONE is on this shit and if you don't know about it you are basically a trucker hat with a mullet that listens to The Red Hot Chili Peppers.

Okay, the left gives us this out-of-hand hot girl who is sick of being hot and just wants to fuck around with her friends and the other one (you can't really see it in this picture but I was there) is wearing heels so high her ass is basically pushed out on a silver platter. It's enough to make you feel sorry for your dick.

The furrowed brow, James Dean pose has got to go. It's so affected and humorless it makes you look like the drummer of Metallica looking at a picture of Erik Lavoie.

What is with British thirtysomethings who work in marketing companies going to music conferences with fucking logos on their shirts like they're teenage snowboarders from the early 90s who listen to De La Soul?

Your dad is supposed to tease you when you talk about shoes too much or play pool so soft the white ball doesn't even make it over there. If he doesn't, you're basically looking at this. Nice going progressive dad. You made a Timmy.

What the fuck is with these hard-case knapsacks people in the tanning-salon community are using? What is in there that can't get damaged—a china toilet seat? Get a regular bag, fag. I think your *Vanity Fair* and your daily planner can handle the odd bonk.

Okay we've been pro small shorts in the past. "Take back the Caucasian cut" and all that but here's something: what the fuck were we talking about? A man's inner thigh is the worst thing bodies can do and we don't need to see any more of it, ever. It's like the opposite of a tit.

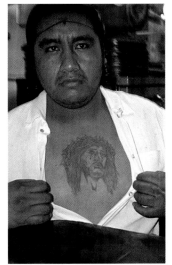

Are poor people into Jesus because he's like, "It's okay to be poor" and that makes them feel better about themselves—or are they poor because they grew up with Jesus and it felt like he'd think they were being lame if they tried to make money?

Often when I commend a woman's outfit I talk about how fun it would be to take it off and how horny it makes us, etc. I don't know if I'm becoming a fag or what, but it would be a shame to take off her clothes. It would almost be more fun to go karaoking and stuff first.

You may find this hard to believe but there is a percentage (a very tiny percentage) of men out there that have never had their asses kicked. Somehow they've slipped through the cracks and see no problem chilling with the kids, listening to Mary J. Blige, and asking 19-year-old girls which glasses he looks better in, "These?" (holds for a pose) "Or these?" (again with the fucking glasses pose).

There is nothing more infuriating than seeing some cunt cop go up to an innocent child in Kansas City and start searching him for crack. WTF lady? Are you insane? The only thing more disgusting than her bullshit harassment was the fact that he had about 40 vials in his socks and was out of his fucking mind on the shit. Ooops.

It's not cool to admit this but the reason boys like girls in high heels is the pain and suffering stilettoes bring. If you're not feeling up for that, we'd honestly rather just see you in Chucks or flats. Compromising with comfy, chunky heels is like wearing a ball gag with a breathing hole.

Dude, what is with the fucking attitude. You are in a *cowboy costume*. Understand? A. Cow. Boy.

Pride can get a bad rap. White pride isn't very popular because it's like, duh. But to be proud of the fact that you are a "Canadian, lesbian, clown, adult" is like being proud to be a "red button" or a "security guard arguing with his friend."

Don't you get the feeling a lot of white kids in the rap scene are trying to be something they're not? The way they talk and dress and their mannerisms and the shoe polish on their faces and all that. It's like they want to be black or something.

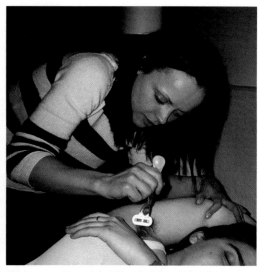

You know a girl is a fucking babe when you fantasize about being her poo.

This is a rare picture of the "Clean Up College Girls Collective," a group of volunteers that go around dosing first-year feminists and then shaving their armpits, legs, and vaginas. Once all the hair is collected, it's going to be put together in a huge ball and called "gross."

When I first saw this guy, I walked up to him and said, "What are you, a Mad Max Joe Dirt?" and then he just whipped open his jacket like this and light shot everywhere and I went "aaoorghorrrh" like the Nazis in *Raiders of the Lost Ark* when they opened that sacred thing.

Hey! You got your paki nerd on my hip-hop thug! And you got your hip-hop thug on my paki nerd! You stupid fuckin'...whoa, wait a minute—this is delicious!

It's really important to guys that women stay positive, that they don't complain. If he hits you, you have to understand that you were probably being lippy and he's only trying to make sure that it doesn't happen again. Don't cry about it. Be happy that he cares.

Is it weird that I feel like taking a shit on his legs?

One of the best things about hip hop is it made it OK for men to hang out in maternity wear. It's like you're being tucked in everywhere you go.

When you see a girl in a baseball hat it's either some pasty Sorority chick doing her laundry on a Saturday or it's some goddess from Milan that flew down here just to do shots with you. Guess which one this is.

Yeah, we talk about high heels and Chuck Taylors and how we can't get it up when you wear sandals or paint your toenails blood red and then this comes along... Why the fuck do boys like girls in storm boots? We don't fucking know but holy shit, are those jizz-proof?

"Sometimes my daughter will ask me why I spend so much of my time sewing and I just look at the stupid bitch and go, 'It's Maiden, Veronica, can you wrap your tiny, ten-year-old brain around that? No? Then shut the fuck up.'"

This is what sucks about America. While everyone is having a burrito special from Sally's at their desk, Italians are getting so drunk and stuffed during their four hour lunch break that they walk back to work doing upside-down farts.

OK, new type of favorite chick. Sorry, "girl camping" and "girl riding a bike with a basket full of stuff." We loved you last year but our new favorite is "girl who just got back from the dance floor." With her cheeks all flushed and her bangs all wet! I better pull my pants up before dude rats me out.

What happened to Britney? She's not even a MILF. She's a MIWBTSTFBSAMWVW (Mother I Would Be Too Scared To Fuck Because She's A Methhead With Venereal Warts). I feel like she just left me and my little brother alone in the house because "Mommy wants a cocktail."

Hey guy, will you take it easy with the platinum skateboard medallion and the Obey shirts and the wool hats and the fucking Skecher's logos and the Sprite ads and the dunks and all that? You're beginning to look like a cartoon on the front of a box of Sugar Frosted Cool Pops.

What are you, the dude from The Circle Jerks? Let the dreads go, dude. You're bald. We know you love your hair but if you love something set it free.

This looks like that Greek Myth where what's-her-name eats a pomegranate in Hades and then Satan gets to own her after that—only this looks about 8,000 times scarier.

I wanted to hate this guy for pretending to be such a man of the people and then selling them crap tracksuits for ten times their worth, but then I noticed he dresses like a toddler and I couldn't help but be like, "Aw fuck it. He's only three."

Professional dancers have got to go. They're always wiggling around like they have to go pee, even when they're at the dinner table. Then "Ring My Bell" comes on and they lean over going, "I don't know how you can sit still like that." Get the fuck away from me, snakey man.

Harley has such a stranglehold on the fuckin' biker scene it's nice to see some bitches rocking a Suzuki without a second thought. That's more than heavy metal. That's punk rock.

This douchebag has been sleeping on my brother's couch for THREE MOTHERFUCK-ING WEEKS. After considering every punishment from chopping him in half with a Samurai sword to simply raping him, I came up with a doozy. I'm going to let him live out his miserable shit sack of a life.

After making a killing with Céline Dion and shady hydroelectric power, Quebec has decided to export its greatest treasure: raver soccer moms. Now you can not get a boner anywhere you want in the whole world!

"I'll tell you something. I was bored in that marriage because it was going nowhere. I was a human *doing*, not a human *being*. I love my daughter, so help me God, but I was sick of being jealous of her. This way I can be myself, a true artist. I had to leave my family to become my family. Now I'm me *and* my wife *and* my daughter AND I DON'T NEED THEM ANYMORE!!! Fuck the courts."

OK it's good to give bums change and everything. We're all for that but please, please, please, stop painting your toenails blood red. It is freaking us out. Toes are intense enough looking without you drawing that much attention to them. It's like putting lipstick on your labia and nipples or me putting it on the head of my knob.

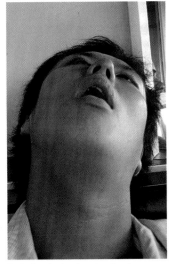

Dude, I understand you barely got any sleep last night (and even if you did, a 12 hour shift at The Peach Pit is exhausting) but you are scaring me. Can you please close your eyes when you sleep? You're making me feel like Pol Pot.

Ah ha ha. You don't bust out a cold compress when your buddy is puking, you fucking Tim. You're supposed to keep asking him if he wants "a greasy pork sandwich dipped in hot whiskey" until he pukes again. Then you laugh your ass off. We thought that was a given.

This guy looks like that time in 2050 when you were totally fucked because the brain police chased you down into the basement of this old furnace factory and there was no way out and you were like, "This is it. I'm fucking dead" and then HE appears out of some weird hole and says, "Follow me!" because he knows the sewers like the back of his hand and the next thing you know you're both firing out of there in a 10-ton bulldozer with the bad guys going, "What the fuck!?" and shooting at you frantically (to no avail).

Am I the only person in the world that gets really horny when he sees a necklace made of babies fucking (with about half doing a 69)? Who hasn't had that fantasy a million times?

While everyone else refuses to go out tonight because they're "pooped," this tenacious little D fuckin' slaps together her summeriest outfit, plops her broken ankle on a trolley, and zooms right over. She can't be stopped. Stab her with a shiv and she'll show up the next day in a Pucci colostomy bag.

We never really understood trophy wives. What the fuck does a 40-year-old talk about with a 22-year-old? It's not like all women turn into Portuguese housewives after 29. If they're hot young then they grow up to be MILFs that get your jokes, dress flawlessly and take cool photographs.

So he takes "math teacher dad" and he New Yorkifies it by reading *Please Kill Me* on the subway. He's like Professor Heroin Jewboy or something and if you get dumped at two in the morning he's the only guy that will come out and have a beer with you.

What the fuck are you supposed to do when a girl with an ass this amazing decides to base her whole outfit on it? How about you just run away crying?

This guy had us on our knees pissing our pants. He was talking about a collaborative paint jam going on later and we couldn't stop thinking about the exact "eureka moment" he decided to solicit his shitty party idea at the line up of this outdoor party. You should have heard his pitch.

I don't know how this guy looks wandering around in person (someone sent us this from London), but as far as pictures go, we're in. It's like disco terrorist meets the Tamil Tigers. I guess the only kind of shoes you could wear with this are high-top white Chucks, so let's just assume it's that and not even think about flip-flops.

Thank God you're broke. When a woman takes "ghetto stripper" to an art show and has the ass out like that, you know you are willing to spend every penny you can to make her happy. When that means a house and a car it's kind of pathetic, but when you're buying her a beer with change and butting in line to get her cheese it's kind of romantic.

Rat tails used to be rad because they told everyone that you used to have long hair but you cut it off and moved on BUT you will never forget when you had long hair. Now they're rad because they show everyone that you used to be around when people had rat tails but you cut that part of your life out and moved on BUT you will never forget when people had rat tails.

That's it baby. Eat that big sandwich. Oh yeah, you love it. You love eating that sandwich. Oh you're good. Uh. Oh - Jesus Christ. Hng!

As you get older, you can break out the sweatpants or you can keep forcing the square peg of staying young into the round hole of aging. The former is a bum-out (literally), and the latter is expensive and painful and, eventually, very disturbing. Why not take a whole new fucking route? Right out there. Why not get on some crazy international, multicultural space thing where you're way too out there to look like you're trying to do anything?

Holy shit, it's a *This Is Your Life* babe. She has the Linda Ronstadt hair your babysitter had in the 70s, the Olivia Newton-John pants your friend's sister had in the 80s, and that Gwen Stefani top your first girlfriend had in the 90s. You've been jerking off about this girl for 25 years.

Hey, what the fuck are they doing? Are they serenading 12-year-olds!? What are they going to do, take the girls out for a romantic night on the town and then split their pelvic bones in half? Dude, they can barely get a tampon in there—understand? That's why there's a law.

There is nothing worse than Wall Street guys that ride Harley's and dirt bikes. It makes you just want to stretch a sharp wire across Park Avenue and watch all their customized helmets go flying through the air like popcorn as your friends pick up the headless bodies and start dancing like it's *Weekend at Bernie's*.

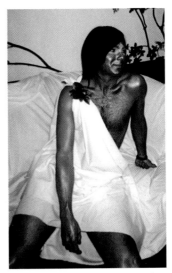

Our new pet peeve starting right now is safety kids. Whatever happened to getting a cut? Can we not make some BMX jumps and have some double dares please? If we have to see another parent lug around bags of sunscreen and hats and helmets and, whatever the fuck these things are, Water Joggers? We are going to make him eat a spider and give him the most severe purple nurple of all time.

What could be more disturbing than a nude nerd buying a Snapple? We don't want to look at your spindly spider legs you fucking gross little man. And the thought of your greasy little dick hiding behind your Manhattan Portage man purse just made me throw my hot dog in the garbage. Thanks.

When I showed my Scottish dad a bunch of pictures from this body painting toga party he said, "What a bunch of pooves" and I laughed for about an hour at the pluralization.

When we did an issue of the magazine dedicated to a random French Canadian named Erik Lavoie (for no reason whatsoever), it made everyone so confused that God came out of the sky and invited us to his house. We got really stoned with him and glued a bunch of shit to the walls and even Evil was there being all wasted. It was intense.

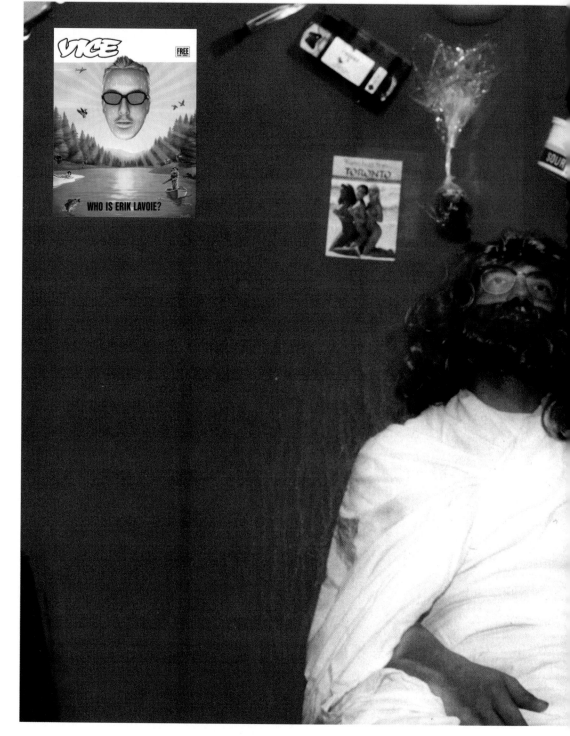

That GBH 80s mohawk look may seem a little passé now but it's so flawless you feel like you could prove it's aesthetic appeal using a calculator. The big sole shoes with massive cuffs provide a pedestal for a barrage of shit that gets crowned by a big do at the top? That's how buildings are designed (fact).

When every woman at this thing was trying so hard her heels were sticking into the grass and her make-up was streaming down her face, funny cute chicks like this would stroll by like a buddy with a vagina and you'd be like, "I do."

If this was a wigger or a fat 12-year-old this hat would get on our nerves but I think the guy is Filipino or Korean or something and that makes the whole big tit thing work (sorry if that's racist). The Lavoie glasses are a nice touch.

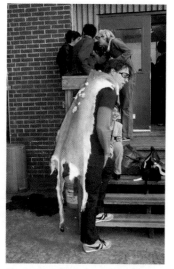

These 70s high school shorts are going to be the death of all Western males this summer. Terry towel ones, Howe lee sheet. Can you invent some split crotch ones so we can do it without you taking them off?

I'm usually not into the whole San Francisco, post punk, skulls and stars stuff (see DON'Ts) but she's kind of really good at it. Maybe it's the Erik Lavoie glasses or maybe it's the fact that I can't see if she's wearing creepers but we're going to bend the rules for this one.

Wearing the pelt of an endangered species is so fucking evil that it goes full circle and becomes rad. Especially when you accessorize it with flowers on the back and a medallion made of hot girl on the front. The Erik Lavoie glasses are the cherry on the sundae.

What is it with British people and their need to have "a look." They're like, "I'm going to be a post grunge hippie in a wool hat no matter how fucking hot it gets." Dude, you are going to go bald in that thing. Please take it off. You're making *my* head itch.

The problem with Rob Zombie is he brought "self-obsessed goth rave" over to "race car redneck" and made a sad contradiction that only makes sense in Florida gay bars. I can't tell if this guy wants to kick my ass or fuck me or both.

Here's a Fisher Price version of that guy. He doesn't want to fuck you or beat you up. He just wants to go to a rave with the rest of the gang from *Toy Story*.

Dreads look fucking bad, but short, newly formed dreads are even worse. Some assholes overheard us say that and have decided the only way to gain our respect is to validate them by having them for five years and growing them to the ground. What is this fucking *Best in Show*?

Sometimes people just keep adding on thing after thing until they look like a window display on St. Mark's. Like a punk version of *Cirque de Soleil* only without the balloons.

"Fuckin' party dude. I am ready to bring it on. Dude, check this. I'm a fucking events coordinator for Tylenol!!! Ha ha! Would you ever have guessed that in a million years? I'm telling you guy, I'm a chameleon! I can go to the game and cheer the Lakers to the playoffs and then—bang—I can bust out the oranges and go to a rock and roll festival!"

When most people wear a T-shirt over a dress shirt they look like a CEO who just showed up for the end of the Fun Run because he wanted to be in the company pictures. When this is the CEO and the Fun Run is a benefit for Eddie, everything becomes a beautiful magical place.

Hearing Erik Lavoie DJ is pure joy. So good in fact, you will see every other DJ in the place just sort of bow his head down in shame. Kudos to those poor bastards for having the respect and insight to know when they are beaten.

There's a certain look that famous punk guys' girlfriends have that nobody else does. Joe Strummer's wife looked like this at the beginning. It's like a weird-for-life / you-will-never-fuck-me-but-everyone's-cool-with-it vibe that is pretty hard to duplicate.

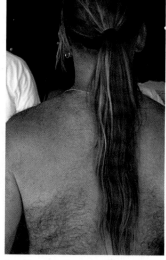

Every rose has its thorn and every party has its animal and where the fuck would this party have been without the guy who came back from "We Greeks invented democracy!" with "Yeah, you also invented homos"?

Speaking of homos, we used to laugh at hairy backs but since the gays brain-washed all the normal guys into shaving their chests and gelling their hair (see any episode of *Real World*) we kind of admire the Conan look. It's become punk.

What is it with rich kids from LA jumping on the Erik Lavoie band wagon? Oh yeah, I know what it is, it's fucking great. The glasses give the whole punk rock chic thing an air of dignity so she can show us her tits and act like a brat but still command the respect of the Erik Lavoie set.

We appreciate the shout out to Erik Lavoie's hometown but slow the fuck down buddy. You are more French Canadian than a mime on third generation welfare. I have to admit however, listening closely to a giant bone you use to shade yourself from the sun isn't French or Canadian or anything anyone's ever seen before. That's all yours.

Go ahead and remove the Sesame Street rave clothes! You think that deP.L.U.R.s him? Wrong! This nigga is down 4 life. Tribal tattoos and a crazy beard are not the markings of a weekend warrior. This guy kicks it 24-7-365. Oh wait, you're not a 14-year-old Italian girl with glow sticks in her hair, you don't give a shit.

Want me to go on a camping trip with an ex-con that killed fifteen people? No problem. Want me to spend two weeks in a pitch black haunted house with nothing to eat but peeled grapes? When?
You want to talk scary? How about a guy that gets Osh Kosh B'Gosh patterns from the library and uses his *Star Wars* sheets to make it happen? That is so fucking creepy it makes you want to glue your underwear shut forever.

This is the San Francisco we love to hate. Punk nerds. They think a massive shower of Confederate / vatos, Eddie Cochrane, Rancid, and The Murder City Devils, is going to wash away a childhood drenched in *Star Trek* and Prince.

Even if you did that with a marker we'd go, "Dude." Who would waste their time with a marker doing such a mediocre joke?" BUT A FUCKING TATTOO!!?? Who are you? Scott Peterson? You're scarier than the fucking overalls guy.

Dear South Beach / L.A. / Bungalow 8, dickehead macho asshole fuckface homophobe that dresses like a fag and shaves his arms. You are a disgrace to that Lavoie face and everything it stands for. You are the anti-Lavoie. A heretic and a penis and if you didn't look so much like The Great One, you would have been killed a long time ago.

You kind of get the feeling that this guy is a total heavy-metal expert who can explain the evolution of Metallica through a Marxist dialectic and goes to Thai cooking classes with Alex Van Halen.

Most men want their kids to be boys because they feel like wimps picking up their girls from figure skating while the guy with strong sperm is picking up his four sons from hockey practice, but what if she was like this? You guys could listen to records together.

This hat is great and everything, but if P.O.D. were playing in the background all "Boom! Here comes the Boom! Ready or not, here comes the boys from the South," it would be intense. It would make you feel like starting a gang with him (or her).

Whatever happened to short shorts anyway? These shits are killing us over here. You should have seen her dancing. She was all 60s'd out and it was too much.

Ties are good because they take a while to get ready. Unlike those shameless cocksuckers running around in sandals, tie people know the dangers of wreckless self-indulgence.

In an era when we're all buying duct tape because we're scared of sand-nigger farts, it is pretty refreshing to see a guy who had a million dollar bounty on his head chilling with a glass of wine and a tape recorder in his face.

Whoa! What is with the bravado, dude? Usually Jewish Egyptian gladiator nerds have a little more humility.

Mules are finally here in full force and we are beside ourselves with joy. Some girls used to complain that it got too cold to wear them at night but now that the 80s sock thing is a possibility there are no more excuses. Get your mules on now! We've got coconuts to smash.

People who grew up with older brothers never went through that awkward phase with the tiny combat boots and the over-sized Siouxsie and the Banshees shirt because their big brother was there to say, "Don't wear that." That's why you asked your Mom for a big brother every Christmas. Little did you know she was infertile. You made her cry you ass.

The boots are rad but how about that fucking shirt? If that was your girlfriend you'd do push ups all the time and get up early to read *The New York Times* just to kind of stay almost worthy.

You know that song by Cutting Crew where he goes, "I could die in your arms tonight"? Even if she's a lez we could work something out. I'll shave my chest and put my dink between my legs or something.

You know how there's certain revealing shirts where you can kind of make out the tits? Imagine if, just once, the girl's shirt was like, "what? these?" and bang. There they were.

This guy is dressed as that chick in Le Tigre that dresses up as a guy. What is he, a punk rock version of God?

The best part of looking at the worst tattoo in the world is, you get to try to figure out his message. Is he saying that he likes aliens, or he is an alien, or just that he believes in aliens? Maybe he's just saying that he has the mind of a little boy.

It's the most self-explanatory DON'T ever made. If you haven't seen your dad in a long time, don't bother finding him. He's wearing a gold hoop earring and has a knuckle tattoo that says "Ozzy."

You know what your aunt thinks you're talking about when you say something is "really cool"? She's not thinking of going swimming on acid or having anal sex to Black Flag. She's thinking of this guy. This is the height of coolness in the aunt community.

Can I fucking smash this with a sledge-hammer? I don't even need protective eye-wear or anything. I *want* to get shards in my face. I want to be covered in blood when I smash this motherfucker to pieces in front of the artist's family.

Shorts on a motorbike is bad enough—I can't wait 'til the exhaust-pipe burns you both—but sandals!? That means every time he goes up a gear, he has to push his big hairy toes against the clutch. How am I supposed to sleep at night with that image in my head?

This chief was so fucking proud of this shirt, we almost thought he knew it looks like a Mexican drug dealer's favorite chair. That's how you know something's really bad. When you think the guy might just be really funny.

How good is that red sweatband? With the coat? No wonder she's smiling like God just gave her the right to become invisible and fly (with a special force-field so she can't die from running into things).

Maybe some of the songs she sings are like "Anchorage" by Michelle Shocked but you can't hear it because you're staring at those stupid fucking shoes the whole time thinking, "are those for reaching things?"

The only thing worse than fake tits is the guys that like them. Grab your ankle and pull it up to your ass. Now push on the side of your calf. That's what they feel like. Gross, eh?

When dudes get laid too much they get this weird vibe about them where they seem kind of like an erect penis — you know what I mean? They're all greasy and shit.

Way to take everything guys like (high heels, tattoos, little vests, tight pants, punky stuff) and just fucking blow it through the ceiling. Slow the fuck down there. It's like getting a blowjob before you can get it up.

You probably don't know what I'm talking about but I fucking HATE these smug reporter types that have pictures of their kids on their laptop (you see it on the plane) and have this really pretentious way of sizing up the political climate of the day with lines like, "The apple doesn't fall far from the Bush."

Dude, *Legacy of Brutality* was great and everything but that was OVER A QUARTER OF A CENTURY AGO. I don't care how many Japanese people still buy your toys, you are almost 50-years-old.

We all know how much Dads hate tattoos but how the fuck can you be mad at a dolphin (with a tattoo of its own) taking a fucking bong hit?

When German tourists visit and try to look American it's corny. When they keep it traditional and stick to the aesthetics of their homeland (like these lederhosen) it's fucking hot. Like when a Japanese chick comes to the party in a kimono.

It's good to see old-time Southerners up in New York DJing and having a good time with the kids. It kind of shows we're all in the same boat and we all know how to have a party time.

If you're lucky enough not to go bald when you're older keep your hair trim and add a small beard. Chicks like it because you become a handsome version of their father and you get to kind of ride the coattails of the 23 years he spent telling her what to do.

It's cool when you go to China and you see people that grew up with no American TV or anything and their look is unlike anything you've ever seen before. When it happens here it's even better.

Body language is as crucial a part of style as any clothes you put on. This slight kink of the hip shows the person is happy to be there and not wrecking it all by being too serious.

No disrespect if you're a retard, but do you hate getting laid? Girls don't go for guys with hiked up baggy track pants because they think it means he's going to have tiny, smelly balls. If you have those at least give them a Wet Wipe and put on some relatively tailored pants for fuck's sakes. Goddamnit!

I'm sorry but that *Animal House* nice-boy thing is impossible to beat. How can you say anything bad about it? It's white and American back when white and American was cool.

Some people look so organized with their look. The same way a skinny, 74-year-old man looks so at home in his straw fedora and yellow slacks, these girls look like they've been dressing like this for a hundred years.

Something tells me this girl has an incredible amount of willpower and would be able to resist you so there's no sense hitting on her. All you can do is make a mental note of her outfit and beg your girlfriend to copy it.

When you have a blazer on and dress according to your income and class you can get away with a lot more boozing than when you "slum it." It's like the difference between an aging clown like John Lydon and a classy boozer like Peter O'Toole.

Hats used to be for funk fans and balding men in denial but we took them back. We started out with those baseball hats that hunters use and then we just took over. I wouldn't be surprised if we took back the top hat and made it good again.

Though Nyah Rock is some sort of ska thing, everyone who sees a T-shirt like this is going to think it's a weird pro-Israel thing. It takes balls to champion the least popular soldiers since the Stalinist purges, and balls are always a DO (unless we're literally talking about testicles, which are gross).

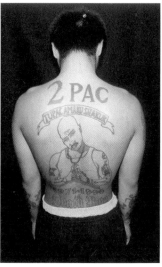

If you want your relationship to last, try to keep things as fresh as the first day you met. Ladies, that means keeping your bush waxed regularly and not lounging around the house in sweatpants all day. Gentlemen, that means not becoming a lazy and fat piece of shit that lets out trombone-sized farts and pisses with the door open.

Dear Japan, we know you all think black people are really cool but Tupac Shakur was an incredibly faggy dancer for Digital Underground that got a gig playing a bad-ass in the movie *Juice* and decided to <u>act</u> that way forever. He is Rob Halford in reverse and you got a fucking tattoo of him.

You're not dickhead Dad. You're "Fun Dad." You listen to The Specials and you open your mouth when you're chewing (eeeew Da-aad!). You even said "shit" once. You so crazy.

Sometimes a guy will meet the wrong girl and his whole life will turn into a bag of shit. Maybe he'd never had anal sex without a condom or something, but this chief is so head-over-heels whipped that she's got him braiding his flaxen hair and wearing eyeliner.

It's a Puerto Rican version of Lenny and Squiggy—grown men dressing like pathetic teenagers (note the hand painted graffiti tag on the boot) and biting their fists every time a pretty girl walks by. I would laugh in their fucking faces if they weren't in a gang.

Hey, look. Terry Richardson and his model girlfriend got zapped with a ray gun that turns everyone into old, ugly, lame versions of themselves. Ha ha. Seriously though, Terry is our boy and whoever did this is going to fucking die.

The thing about Italians is they take care of their mistresses for eternity. Even when the guy dies, he has his son go over there and make sure her radio still works. In exchange, these women stay mind-blowingly hot, right 'til the grave.

This stumbling male prostitute had a credit card in his ass and about $200 in crumpled-up bills in his hands. He looked like a dead ghost and said, "I just came out of a very, very heavy session." So we put the words "oooooh kaaaay" into a bazooka and shot them into outer space.

Call me a prude but is it so suitable to have a little kid Barbie with her tits exposed hanging by a wire around her neck? And who were those socks made for, a four-year-old whore?

Unfortunately, you didn't grow up in a French country. If you did you'd know of a cartoonist named Hergé, his pal Tin Tin, and the GROWN MEN who never got over it. It's the American equivalent of walking around with Mickey Mouse ears but everyone does it.

Ah, finally — everything evil in the world combined into one "my father failed me" moment. We've got: in-the-closet chest-waxing, home embroidery, frat boys, ravers, The Gap, nipple rings, and of course, barefoot dancing on acid.

Adbusters recently had this thing where they're like, "Who's more crazy — the corrupt CEO or the man living on the street?" Er, CEOs may be financial terrorists and everything, but they don't take a cell-phone-sized shit in the middle of the fucking sidewalk.

Nor do they fall madly in love with a slightly chubby, invisible Tinkerbell who's always giggling and saying flirtatious things like, "Oh stop it - you."

After you haven't had it for about five months, there's nothing like getting a real good fucking. One of those workhorse types that is going to last more than an hour and pummel you so thoroughly the bladder infection feels totally worth it.

You can tell when someone's had the exact same look for 15 years. Dude is so laid-back your girl got fucked by him.

God bless the wasted guys. Those greasy Tecate-drinking hosers who fall asleep with their pants on and eat apples out of the garbage.

I'm no fag, but when you see a cute loner guy with great style in Nike Uptowns and a parka you're like, "Maybe I'd let him lick my balls."

Not too nuts about dreadlock soldier on the right, but striped socks is killing shit. Her whole little black package is out of control — she's one of the few Brooklynites that doesn't look out of place in Manhattan.

Denim suits may not be a big deal on the farms of Nebraska, but in the galleries of New York it's the sign of a good drunk.

It's all cool to sit down and enjoy a delicious sandwich after a hard day's drinking, but c'mon. Can we at least finish what's in our mouth? Jeesh.

These girls make getting dressed to go out almost better than going out. You can almost hear the "Sussudio" blaring as they try on their 40th version of the look they call "space slut coke detective."

"I don't need a quarter for the phone nor do I need two dollars for a short bus ride to visit my kids. The truth is, I'm a homeless alcoholic guy that would really like to get more drunk." We liked his honesty so much we threw five bucks out the window which he then ran on to the highway to get. Honesty and safety are not friends.

Speaking of no bullshit, if you're in a cock slump you might as well cut the shit and get the word out there. "I am a gay man and I'm looking for a dick to suck."

Not being ashamed to shave your back is pretty good. Shaving your back so people can see your gang's tattoos is much better but having a slightly post pubescent Spanish girl do it next to an open fire hydrant in the middle of the street is so good it's fucking performance art.

Some things you don't know include: the girl on the left is wearing a homemade head band that says "I love coke," they had just poured a beer on a guy for trying to fondle them, and it doesn't get any better than this.

The Wawa one is pretty nice but how about fucking Leon Spinks at the lowest point of his life? "I lost my wife, I lost my home, I even lost some teef!" is on your arm forever.

Laaaaaame! Guys, that doesn't even look like cum. What is that toothpaste? You're supposed to beat off into a condom and then feed it into his ass with a pencil. Or piss into a glass and then carefully pour it on his crotch. This toothpaste shit is an embarrassment to the "fucking with the passed out guy" profession.

Don't miss this moment, guy. *Santana Live* is blaring and it's your favorite song. This is a rare opportunity to show the bar how fucking bad ass you look when you do this in your living room. Take your 15 minutes and just, fucking, rock it!

Please tell me this is a European. How could a North American woman wear an ass flap with the word "pussy" embroidered on it? What does that even mean anyways, "I'm a wimp that likes to be eaten out"?

Guy, The Flash was the fastest man alive. You're a fat pig with a faggy dog. Get a shirt with food on it or something. Right now you're a parody of how slow you are.

Not only were these guys saving up their fishnet undergarments 'til the end of the party but they grabbed their nuts and gave them a real good hard jostling for all to admire when they did.
So it's 6 AM and we're high as shit with nothing to drink or look at but a pair of fishnet balls. How's that for a downer?

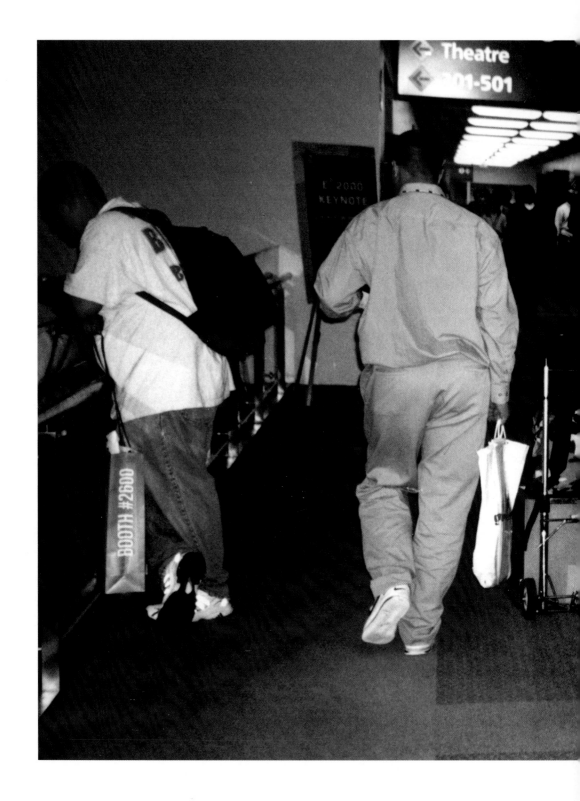

Who the fuck are these people? Are they five years old? Do they have a fort under the stairs and curse the streetlights for coming on because it means bedtime. Do they "hate Craig's guts?"

OK you know those guys know they look kind of cool. That outfit *has* to tap into the little kid in them that used to dream of being some kind of heavy duty SWAT team supercop. If he doesn't even have a hint of that in the back of his head I don't know or understand anything about anything.

Britney Spears obviously has something. Kids like her. Old people like her. Even we like her. If she has something that special don't fight it—surround yourself with it any way you can. It will rub off on you.

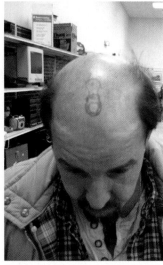

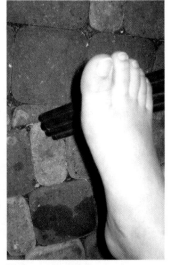

You can't really go wrong with mod clothes. They're a timeless combination of sharp hipness and virgin innocence. The kind of thing that goes really well with gigantic bazooms.

"My ex wife said I was an open book and I said 'Fuck that Carol, I'm an open beer' and that's when I decided to get a beer tab tattooed to my head. Of course, I was pretty shitfaced at the time."

When you see a girl who wears pumps a lot the odds are her toes are mangled pieces of machinery. Then they throw on some crazy blue polish and it's like seeing a clown in a car wreck. That's why it's so refreshing to kick off a girl's stiletto and see this little piece of food sitting there, untouched. Yum.

There are approximately three types of "kooky guys." There is the gay dude that just got dumped and has decided to "reinvent himself" by dumping all his old friends, hanging out in a new neighborhood, and dressing like Malcom McLaren's grandson on Halloween.

Then there's the small-dicked jock that has decided the only way to get laid is to stick out in girls' minds as much as possible. He's really fun at parties if you're a stupid asshole.

And finally, there's the guy whose dad is a priest and who took "no matter what anyone says you have to have faith in your beliefs and be your own person" way past religon and into hippie faggot pig boy from outer space.

Similarly, there are three types of kooky *old* guys. There is the semi-literate Irish guy that has lots of female friends and tries not to fart at dinner parties.

Then there is the "OK this is my final final FINAL try to get my career going" artist man that spends the rest of his inheritance on a nutty $700 blazer that will stick in the head of curators and make him feel 38 again.

And finally we have the quirky old poof millionaire that has decided to become a caricature of himself and passionately embrace the silly elf man persona he spent so many years trying to avoid.

Whether this guy is a Nigerian president, a 5% Nation of Islam fundamentalist, or simply a loon, we would like to offer up a raging five-star review. Have you ever seen more poise in your life?

Who said heroin chic is dead? You could be behind her right now spooning up a storm. You could be caressing her arms and picking at whatever scab was ready to go. How is that not chic? What are you AIDsophobes?

You haven't experienced Tupac and 50 until you've seen them drawn by a Lebanese art student. Take your pick, yo. You can have 50 Cent's rage in a myriad of pastel markers or you can see what Tupac would look like as a Somalian lesbian.

How long have you been pissing for? A quarter of a century? And you still can't fucking work your genitalia? We don't know if it's low IQ bitches that think venereal warts live on toilet seats or if it's self-obsessed jocks but mark my words, we are going to find you pissers on lids. And when we do we are going to make you drink so much of our piss you'll have to undo your top button.

"I've got four kids. My wife doesn't want to fuck me anymore and I don't want to fuck her. My only friend is my brother (like he gives a shit). So, fuck it. You can all have a big long stare at my hideous demeanor. My whole body is giving you the finger."

Black teenagers should not be allowed to read comic books. They get way too into it and next thing you know they're "fighting crime" and standing on dangerously high support beams calling you "Encromeda."

Yeah, he's just a typical Southerner cleaning up some trees in his front yard, right? Wrong! He's a tough-as-nails war vet with a motherfucking pet mountain goat that watches his every move. And you slept on how great he is. FUCK YOU!!!

We caught her waiting for her friend in the park and there was a weird vibe that maybe she knew we were trying to stealthily photograph her and she knew she had a great outfit on and she knew it had to be documented.

DOs & DON'Ts

Ugly redheads can do a lot of shit to make up for the fact that nobody likes them. They can be funny or start a band OR they can redefine what aesthetics are and go out in elaborate costumes every night. Now who's handsome—bitch?

You can have all the mistresses with all the cleavage and crazy purses you want. We're going to stick to the casual Sunday girl with her really scuffed up leather boots and then, like, some shirt that was on the floor.

Enough with the L.E.S. posers and their frilly jackets. These niggas are the real deal. Wouldn't it be cool, if you were really rich and you paid them to totally decorate your apartment? Fuggin' black panther statues and landscape paintings, how authentic would that be?

Whoa, it's the walking police sketch. Did you purposely set out to look like the personification of rape or is that a look that sort of just toppled out of the closet onto your head?

One of the really great things about dark pants is they take attention away from what might be percieved as a big ass and they keep the eyes up top, where the tits are.

He was angry because she took off his glasses and smashed them on the sidewalk and she was angry because he was trying to get her boyfriend arrested for spitting on a lady. We were angry because we were laughing at these babies so hard we got stomach pains and couldn't take enough pictures (jerks).

This fucking chief kept insisting we take a picture of him. After we got a good shot of him and his piss stained pants he insisted we mail him a copy of the print. When we told him it's digital and asked for his email address he said "I'm going to be on a DVD?" so we walked away worrying about humanity.

The only thing worse than a guy passed out in a chair is an old nude guy passed out in a chair in the freezing cold right after a devastating hour in the hot tub. He had steam rising off him like an alcoholic dumpling. It was terrible.

"Goddamnit Marcus, you take the car without asking and you don't even look inside to see if your Father's coat is in there. Shit! Now I'm forced to wear this ridiculous thing ... Where the fuck is he anyways?"

And just when she thought she was going to be lonely forever, a tactless Jewish man neglected to tell her he's married and convinced her to hold him close and rub his area outside the gallery.
She keeps emailing nudes of herself and he keeps shuddering.

She's into black dudes because her golf-obsessed ex-husband never ate her ass. He's into white girls because he's black. Together they have sex that's so raunchy it makes 18-year-old homeless prostitutes gasp in disbelief.

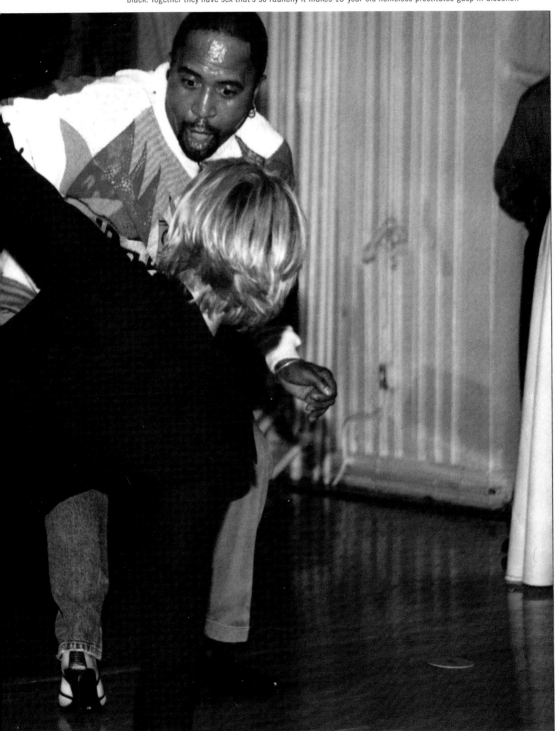

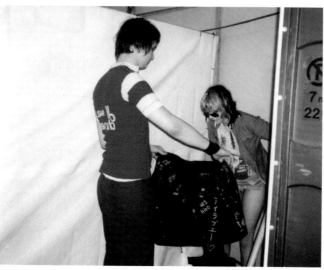

Hey lesbians, why you gotta hate? We're not all bad. Some of us are perfectly able to stop talking to our friends for a minute and go help a woman remain decent when she goes. I was there BTW and the guy didn't even look at her during the main part. He did threaten to kick my ass after this picture was taken however but that's good too.

When Japanese girls dress the same they look like wimps. When white girls do it it's like two exclamation marks!! Pow!! I am now officially totally into colored tights and I wouldn't have known that if they hadn't hammered it home in double whammy fashion.

Okay, I photoshopped out the lip piercing and now she is totally, 100% perfect. With those huge Gazelle glasses and the hat like that, can you imagine how well she dances?

Graffiti gets on my fucking nerves but this is amazing. It's like a Basquiat fuck you finger but with amazing cartoon balls.

Gay bars are filled with incredibly hot, straight girls that dress crazy and want to go somewhere their overwhelming hotness won't lead to lecherous drunks leaning over them all night. If you go there you will get so horny your pants will rip.

Don't get me wrong, heroin is great and everything but what the fuck is the matter with these people? Hey Dorothy, just because you build a living room on a park bench and click your heels three times doesn't mean you're not in the fucking park anymore. You can't just crash. Junkies are the biggest fucking losers in the world. At least drunks say funny shit.

We're not sure what happened to electroclash. Everyone was into it (even us) and then it seemed to morph into a weird kind of drag queen talent show thing and now look at it.

Look at these turds. Could they be bigger pieces of human waste please? Look at them. They're just two big pieces of genitalia with ridiculous hats on. They're not even worth diarrhea-ing on.

Er, if you're going for medieval biker punk you might want to get something a little more substantial than a fucking Vespa. Those are for a type of in-the-closet girly man we call a "mod." When you ride it you look like elephant Satan going to battle on a tricycle.

Shhhhh, don't awake the sleeping Jew. Washing and drying his four foot long hair can take all morning so cut the guy some slack and let him rest.

When picking up guys it's important to let them know you are a libidinous woman that respects the guy's body and wants to explore him (even his toes).

Recently we've noticed girls are wearing everything in the world at the same time. It creates an effect called "partying" and often leads to another thing called "fun night."

You know when you get really baked and you do a funny dance thing around the living room that makes your sister laugh so hard she pees herself? Some people like that moment so much they decide to do it forever.

If you see a guy in a bar with perfect tits that looks like he might be a go-er, don't be a pussy and sit there staring at him all night. Go up there! Rub your dick against his bare ass until he notices you.

Nothing looks better than someone about to get into a fight. Everything about you looks totally on purpose. Even a big beard and a trucker hat makes perfect sense.

Of course, if you get the living shit kicked out of you it's not quite so amazing. You know what? It's probably best to stick to the *going to fight* look and just try to avoid the whole *having just fought* look.

Ah ha ha ha ha. Look at his fucking tattoos. A belly button tribal sun (which is essentially saying, "Pay attention to my stomach") and a motherfucking grandfather clock?! What are we, in Turkey?

What is it with Puerto Ricans where they're perpetually ten years old? Oh yeah, they don't have a dad.

Naked ladies are pretty, even to people that aren't sexually attracted to women. However, having a woman spread her gash on your back for the rest of your life is totally fucking insane. How white trash are you? Did you grow up in the garbage?

Who's in the mirror, Carl? Do you see a funky version of Steve Tyler? Do you see an irreverant rocker that does the wango tango?
Give up the bass, dude. You're old.

Who says you need whores to be a pimp? Pimpin' is a state of mind. You can be a pimp about how you do your homework or how you help your Dad move his office. Some of the biggest pimps in the world haven't even seen a tit.

Owe kaaaaaye. Now I've seen everything. Wallabees with heels. Could you have more of a cake-and-eat-it-too combination, please? What's next, a pretty girl with a brain?

I know it's relaxing to ejaculate (especially when you're drunk), but you might not want to freeze time by passing out for six hours (no joke) when her head is at a 97-degree angle and you're both completely naked on my kitchen floor.

Why couldn't al-Qaeda have cut *this* guy's head off instead? After they were done they could spin it around in the air using that three-foot-long poo dread he's got tucked into the back of his pants.

I hate when people think they're saving the world just by riding their bike. It's like those black and white couples that think they're fighting racism just by fucking each other.

I thought *Ab Fab* was a comedy show that contained exaggerated fictional characters. It seems Jennifer Saunders and Joanna Lumley were only scratching the surface of how limitlessly ridiculous old, ugly, rich, British women can be. It's like Gary Glitter fucked Axl Rose and your mom came out.

"So yeah, after I got kicked out of Crazy Town I was watching TV all drunk one night and I saw all this shit about 9/11 and I was like 'damn!' Now I'm here and I'm fucking doin' something real, you know? I don't need those guys. 'Come My Lady'? That song was bullshit. I got my own shit goin' on right here and it's real. Something important. I don't need L.A. because that just ain't me. I'm a people person. Always have been. I'm at a point here where I want to do something real. Something more than rock and rap or whatever it was called. Something that involves making a change. I mean, I'm still writing. I'm still making music and who knows if that shit will ever happen again but it's not all about that these days. It's about being real and drawing people what you can do. I know what I can do. I can make a difference. Me. AC."

The sores and the constipation are pretty bad but the worst thing heroin does is make men feel so confident and comfortable that on a hot day they have no problem throwing on a soft cotton skirt and flip-flops. He's going to nod out on a park bench soon and we'll all get to see his nuts roasting in the sun.

Why do we love New York so much? I guess because it's the only city on earth with hot dog stands like this.

Is it me or are you noticing a lot more guys wearing Michael Jackson jackets? I couldn't rock something that gay myself but when those guys are around you feel like you're in a Ralph Bakshi cartoon where everyone moves around all smooth-like and you can throw the bouncer through a wall.

I like it when guys shave off their moustache. Their faces look so bald. Remember when your dad would do it after 15 years and you'd be like, "Who the fuck are you?"

Most races are like popcorn kernels. The girls are super hot and sizzling and then, at 30, BANG they puff out to 10 times their size. On the other hand, blacks don't crack and this "Hot Mama" (check the belt buckle) is still so fuckable it makes you wonder why her kids don't beat off thinking about her.

In the 1400s they were called "simpletons" and they did handy things like pick up empty glasses at the local tavern and play the lute. Today illegal aliens clean up our glasses, so the simpletons are left with no recourse but to get so fucking wasted they buy *Black Tail* for the train home and sit there with a boner going, "What?" (Sucks for them but I like it).

Some dude who was at Disneyland sent this to us with the caption, "Not sure if this is a DO or a DON'T." Are you nuts? While every woman in America is too scared to sport anything but a Juicy Couture jumpsuit this Cyndi Lauper supermodel is wearing a fucking bikini on top of a garage sale's worth of great outfits.

Hey shit for brains, didn't you hear the news? Even the gays have renounced male thongs.

Whoa! I can't believe I made fun of those other dudes just for wearing sarongs. It's like the N'Sync cowboy here and his Hawaiian Ninja buddy are staring at us going, "You got a problem?"
(For the record, these are the worst guys in this entire book).

The problem with being British is that you are so naturally ugly that you need a zinger to make a dent. Maybe if you do something kooky like get a Mohawk or dye your hair straw yellow some saddie with beer goggles will mistake it for character.

This guy is a such a haphazard clash of every kind of man on earth (Eminem, The Terminator, Howdy Doody, Schneider, The Village People cowboy) you start to think he's an alien. All of a sudden it's not so fucking funny to laugh at him.

Why be a Glaswegian punk from 1983 when you live on the beach? Dude, have you seen this page? There is 0.00 guy competition. Go put on a normal pair of shorts and collect your harem.

In the summer of 1999 I did the DOs & DON'Ts with Joe Strumer (The Clash). As was said in the intro to the book I feel like he truly got the joke and was one of the few people I could ever see doing a better job than me at this. I was going to will this column to him when I died but he died first.
His comments are in red text and mine are in black.

There's a certain American style of wearing shorts that is absolutely awful, and it's the same as the Spanish men. They stuff their shirts into their shorts with a belt through the loops. It's not on. We call it belt pride. This guy's obviously wearing the same shorts he's had since he was a baby.

That is a really huge basket really. Filled with stuff (maybe). They walk miles in Africa with that stuff on their head and we never developed that ability here in the West.

The guy in plaid is what we call a drum and bass hoser. There's no more rock shows in Canada so they're taking over all the clubs. When we were doing *Earthquake Weather* in 1989 we got addicted to Bob & Doug Mackenzie reruns. It got so that everyone in the control room was a hoser. I've never dropped the use of that word and I never even knew what it meant until today.

This is one of those Jazz-fan type guys that dresses himself 100% based on logic. He's brave, we can say that.

Is he going through that skip? I know how he feels. I can't resist having a look in other people's skip. Bo Diddley and Paco DeLucia have the same obsession. It's a sickness that most guitarists have.

Neeer neeeeeeeeeeeer neeeer bvvvvvf bvvvvvvf. Honk! Honk! Neeeeer neeeeeeeeeeeeeeeeeeeeeeeeeeeeer neer neeeeer neeeeer. Hey watch it pal (swerve)! Neeeeeer neeeeer neeeeeeer. He's really moving that guy. I like the shirt, coming out of the shirt. Full points for that.

I like that breezy white look. Minus the knapsack it's so comfortable, it's sexy. In a sweaty country that would be excellent.

That's nice eh? She's just sitting around thinking hard with that little splash of orange on her pants. I really like the girl picking the fruit on the bicycle. That's a guy and he's wearing sandals. Oh yeah, you're right. I'm blind. You've never needed glasses have you? No. I think I'm on the list. I think I should go to Lenscrafters during my next lunch hour.

I don't blame her for checking herself out like that. That sundae of dark colors with the pink-hair-and-belt cherry on top. 100 out of 100 on that. It's all in the attitude isn't it? We're learning something here.

I like big shoes with floods. It's good—yeah.

This is a guy in Calgary. You can't see it here but he has this really giggly strut like the end of *Saturday Night Fever* in ffwd. Look at his helmet. The guy is tiny.

These knapsacks are getting out of control. Something has to be done. I must say I like the Teletubbies. Something about the way they wobble is really endearing.

Fanny packs are impossible to pull off. OK, we've got a big problem here. It couldn't be worse really. Appalling. And we're the ones that have to look at it. He's medieval but without the panty hose. "Get some hose on you hoser!"

(STONE ROSES VIBER)

CRESSA

Manchester

Illustration by Joe

You can't rock the biker look with fucking sandals. It's hypocrisy. He looks like Lemmy on the beach. That would be a good fashion shoot. Sandals!? The Stone Roses had a vibemaster. A dancer named Cressa that made them rich. He is my sandal guru. He's been the only person that could ever convince me to consider wearing those horrible things. I've been in the most vile conditions with him and he always has them on and they look all right. He says your feet are like your lungs. I'd like to think I could pull that off but I can't. I haven't got the guts.

The shoes are a bit rich but this girl just knows what she's doing. If she wants to fuck you she will. It's not up to you. You know that her pad is in order and the kitchen looks good. There's no filthy piles of newspapers stacked everywhere. She'd cool us down if we were too high on blow. We could stop gripping the table with our teeth and we'd be in an oasis of tranquility. Another 100 out of 100. She's got a real stride going on here with a most difficult footwear apparatus. Sometimes I'm glad not to be a woman because I hate having foot impediments strapped to the end of my extremities. This bird is going very far and moving dead fast.

Dear, MEN OF

PUT SOME FUCKING SHOES ON!!!

LOOK, WE'RE NOT SAYING YOU ALL HAVE TO BE LUMBERJACKS AND RUN AROUND CHOPPING WOOD AND HUNTING OUR FOOD, BUT FOR FUCK'S SAKES!!! THIS ISN'T A FUCKING COLLEGE DORM SO CHANGE OUT OF YOUR PAJAMAS. THE SITE OF YOUR DISGUSTING MAN FEET ARE MAKING US SICK. WHAT'S THE MATTER WITH YOU!? YOU'RE WORSE THAN FAGS! GET A FUCKING JOB AND GET SOME SHOES ON! (feel free to take one of these a hand, if out)

PUT SOME FUCKING SHOES ON!!!
PUT SOME FUCKING SHOES ON!!!
PUT SOME FUCKING SHOES ON!!!
PUT SOME FUCKING SHOES ON!!!
PUT SOME FUCKING SHOES ON!!!
PUT SOME FUCKING SHOES ON!!!
PUT SOME FUCKING SHOES ON!!!
PUT SOME FUCKING SHOES ON!!!
PUT SOME FUCKING SHOES ON!!!
PUT SOME FUCKING SHOES ON!!!
PUT SOME FUCKING SHOES ON!!!

ABOUT THE AUTHOR

Gavin McInnes is a complete asshole that ostracizes everyone he speaks to and dresses like a fucking idiot. He is richer than shit, however, and divides his time between his home in Costa Rica and his apartment in New York.

Um, what else? He was born just outside of London in 1970, played in a bunch of crappy punk bands like Anal Chinook and Leatherassbuttfuk, did a comic book called Pervert for several years and started up VICE Magazine in Montreal in 1994 with Suroosh Alvi and Shane Smith. Today he is sitting outside writing an "about the author" about himself.